SOLOMON GRASSROOT

SOLOMON GRASSROOT

Ann Lindvall Arika

Photos: Lindvall Arika, Ann except Photos 19 and 23
  Photo 19: Permission to publish from Roger Keesing Papers MSS
  427, Special Collections & Archives, University of California San
  Diego, USA
  Photo 23: Permission to publish from Orisi, Wilzen, Solomon
  Islands
Cover: Lindvall Arika, Ann
Publisher: BoD – Books on Demand, Stockholm, Sweden
Print: BoD – Books on Demand, Norderstedt, Germany
ISBN: 978-91-7969-733-4

ACKNOWLEDGEMENTS

With these words, I want to thank *iufala evriwan*, 'all of you', who have helped me make this book come true.

A special thanks goes to Anne-Maree Schwarz, Suzanne Feary – both of them living in Honiara – Jean Hudson and Gloria Webb, who have given valuable comments and suggestions. Thanks also to my *wantoks*, 'one-talk, same language', Björn Svensson and Eva Carlsson, as well as Janet Fenwick, Jean Schellhart, Karen Graybeal, Rosebud Armstrong and Shanti Dorairaju Fowler for the same reasons.

Thanks, Lime Lounge and YWCA, both in Honiara, for their great helpfulness.

Last, but not least, a big thanks to my husband Robert Arika, all my family members, relatives, friends and neighbours for explanations, advice and encouragement.

Taggio tumas, evriwan.
Bao le'a baita, famoru te'efou.

REVIEWS

'I read this book before starting to work in Honiara and it was a great introduction to life in "The Hapi Isles". This is essential reading for anyone who wants a deeper understanding of contemporary life in Solomon Islands.' *Björn Svensson, Australia. Volunteer, Tourism Advisor in Solomon Islands ('The Hapi Isles')*

'I met Ann Lindvall Arika in Honiara in 2012 and again in 2019. Helping her with editing and translating has been a great pleasure and a privilege, not only because it can now be read by a wider audience but because it opened my eyes to so much about Solomon Islands and her people. This book is about her life; how she came to understand and adapt to Solomon Islands culture and society and to flourish in a place that has many challenges. It is the most fascinating, honest and accurate insight into Solomon Islands culture that I have ever come across, and, in my view, should be read by everyone intending to get there. I will be recommending that the Australian Volunteer programme make the book essential reading for future volunteers going on assignment to Solomon Islands.' *Suzanne Feary, Australia. PhD in Archaeology. Assisting the Ministry of Culture & Tourism in Solomon Islands*

'A great "culture guide" with lots of useful dos and don'ts.' *John Berggren, Sweden*

'Ann Lindvall Arika tells us not only what she observes but also how she feels, with honesty and humour ... She has quietly adopted Solomon Islands ways and lives as Solomon Islanders do. If you are a visitor to Solomon Islands, this book will give you additional insights to enrich your own experiences.' *Anne-Maree Schwarz, New Zealand. PhD. Collaborator on Marine Resource Management, Solomon Islands*

'I could not stop reading... Your writing means a lot to me, for it is like scratching under the surface, trying to understand our complex culture. Getting down to the Melanesian mind set can be very difficult for most people of other cultures, but you are able to do it quite well. I congratulate you Ann. I want you to write more.' *Dr. Lazarus Tavichikai, Solomon Islands*

My linguist friend and colleague at Malmö University, Sweden, Ann Lindvall Arika, who has chronicled many of her travels over the years, tells us about everyday life in her adopted country. Her story is about day-to-day happenings enhanced by her own insightful reflections on events and characters in this Pacific nation.' *Jean Hudson, Prof. em. on English Linguistics, Sweden*

'Somewhat the same theme as in *The White Masai* by Corinne Hofmann, but with a different end...' *Lisa Lundqvist, Sweden*

'Why would a highly experienced and world travel writer as Ann Lindvall Arika from Sweden, a developed country, want to marry someone in East Kwaio and spend her entire life in Solomon Islands? – That's my question.' *Julian Maka'a, Writer for Island Sun, Solomon Islands*

'Ann Lindvall Arika's book *Solomon Grassroot* pulled me into a journey into another world. The 'former' picture of the South Pacific is substituted with a new and fresher picture than the one many of us have been 'fed' with. Not only her knowledge but also her experience as a traveller give a new dimension to travelling as an art, with a warm and active participation in other cultures – a travel story which ends up in emigration. The people around her are an important element, where 'Respect' is one of her mottoes. She also touches the negative impacts of the Western World, important to emphasize. I as a reader am really getting even more interested in this part of the world, and the desire to travel is, after this reading, almost irresistible.' *Maria Veneke Ylikomi, Language Consultant, Writer for Maia, former Publisher, Sweden*

'Replanting oneself in new soil is nothing unusual, but doing it in so different soil is unusual. The writer and Ph.D.-linguist Ann Lindvall Arika writes from her and her husband's palm leaf house in Solomon Islands' capital Honiara. She paints house, surroundings, people, animals, daily duties; That is the life in a country where nobody is in a hurry but where everybody has something to do. Interpersonal relations are the important issue, not strive after individual success.

Lindvall Arika sees herself as an ordinary 'grassroot' in a Solomon version. But she is of course not so 'ordinary'. She is a well-educated, European woman who manages the piece feat of neither romanticizing nor give way for exoticism, a balance act which I think few would manage. She is doing it with a maintained integrity. She tells in a simple way how it is; about people around her, and also about political, social and economic conditions in a country, which, as it appears, may have similarities with any old agrarian country. That is the exciting point with her book – to see everyday life so far away, to understand the feeling of home-coming which is the point of departure of the book. The book awakes thoughts about our own society; do we have it best? Ann Lindvall Arika has a personal answer to that question.

Solomon Grassroot is written in a vivid and fresh style. Rich background facts and many photos complete this unusual emigrant story.
Kerstin Gansmark, Culture Reviewer, Sweden

FOREWORD

Solomon Grassroot is a translation and further elaboration of two published autobiographic books in Swedish: *Korallbältet – vresor i Melanesien och Mikronesien* [The Coral Belt – Travelling in Melanesia and Micronesia] 2008 and *Härhemma i Honiara – mitt liv i Salomon-öarna* [Here at Home in Honiara – My Life in Solomon Islands] 2011. Part I is based on the first book covering the years 2006-2007, when I was still travelling. Part II is based on the second book covering 2008-2011, where I mainly depict my own living environment in Honiara and in East Kwaio. Part III covers the following years 2011-2020. Statistics, prices etc. are always from 2020, even in Part I and II.

Then, who am I? I am a Swedish woman and have been based almost all my life in Sweden. (I have travelled quite a lot, though.) Solomon Islands is my new home country and the capital Honiara my new home city. Via my marriage, I have been given a big family, and this book describes everyday life here – mine and theirs – as a Solomon 'grassroot'. My family belongs to the ethnic group Kwaio, living on the east coast of Malaita Island in Solomon Islands. Consequently, I want to give a deeper insight into the Kwaio culture, as well as background facts about the nation as a whole.

The autobiography is an attempt to answer the questions: Why did I take the step? What is everyday life like? What kind of happiness and sorrows do the people have? How do the different cultures meet? Is the culture 'totally different', 'enormously exotic', etc.? How can a foreigner feel at home here? (My friends who emigrated from Sweden to Australia describe their step as a move to the neighbour's house, compared to mine.)

I have tried to be neutral and objective, but still, all my impressions are interpreted through my Swedish eyes; anything else is not possible. But now, come with me and have a look yourself!

TABLE OF CONTENTS

Where Do I Live?

The sun is sending its first rays through the coconut palm and makes the leaves in the walls shine golden yellow. From my mattress I look up to the beautiful woven ceiling. It has been daylight – or *big day* as we say here – for a long time, but as the house here in Koa Hill is shaded by a mountain top, it takes some time for the sun to reach the house. I slip out from the mosquito net, quiet so as not to wake anybody up, wrap a *lavalava*, sarong, around me and go out on the veranda. Pussy is rubbing her body up against me. She is hungry and meows heartbreakingly.

Above the house, the slope rises sharply towards the American Memorial, the monument for fallen US soldiers during World War II. Below the house runs the Mataniko River, having emerged from the mountains behind Vara Creek. The river will continue under the Mataniko Bridge, the bridge that separates Chinatown from Honiara's centre, leisurely pass Chinatown where some Chinese women hang their laundry and some Melanesian men chew *betel nut*, and then end up in the ocean.

Back to the house. On the other side of the river, looking south, dizzying green heights are outlined, and behind them is Guadalcanal in all its mute isolation.

Koa Hill, south-west of Chinatown, is a suburb of Honiara. Honiara is situated on the north coast of the main island of Guadalcanal and is the capital of Solomon Islands. Solomon Islands is situated just under the equator, east of Papua New Guinea and north-east of Australia, far out in the Pacific Ocean.

This is where I live. This is my home.

The way home has been long.

PART I: THE WAY HOME

PART I: THE WAY HOME

First Stop Polynesia

Writing, languages and travelling

Everything in my life has circled around three areas: writing, languages and travelling. So what was more natural than I became a writer of language textbooks, a travel writer and a lecturer in 'International Migration and Ethnic Relations'. And took a PhD in Linguistics.

Almost all of my life I have been based in Lund, a university town in southern of Sweden, characterized by an extensive ethnic and cultural diversity. Early on I was curious to see the world. My compass led me to Europe, Asia, Africa, North and Central America (while South America is still to be done) and, of course, Oceania. If they still stamped the passports, I would count 61 stamps by now.

In 2006 I was planning to get material for my book about travelling in Melanesia and Micronesia. This long journey needed thorough planning. I had to do several stopovers in places where I had been before and fallen in love with, so it suited me well. I had six months to burn. So via Copenhagen, London and New York I started with French Polynesia.

Bienvenue à Tahiti

Around midnight between 1st and 2nd October 2006 I took my first steps on the rain-wet tarmac at Faaa, Tahiti's International Airport. Tahiti is the main island in French Polynesia and the site of the capital Papeete. At the hostel Chez Fifi I threw myself on the bed. Although I was deadly tired, I could not sleep: my mind was racing, thinking about everything. For example, where I was, and where I was heading.

I had been to seven countries in the Pacific: French Polynesia, Cook Islands, New Zealand, Fiji, Tonga, Samoa and Hawai'i, and now I was planning Vanuatu, New Caledonia, Solomon Islands, Marshall Islands, Kiribati and Nauru. I thought that I would cover the Pacific fairly well with 13 countries, until I found out that there are 22! Or rather countries and territories. Not all of them are independent nations, but it doesn't stop them from having a very particular identity. And I thought I had a reasonable idea about Pacific culture as a whole, characterised by a strong social affinity focused on the family and their own ethnic group.

The Pacific, Papua New Guinea, Australia and New Zealand make together up the continent of Oceania. The total population of the Pacific in 2020 was c. 3 million, not including Hawai'i or Easter Island (which are, in spite of indigenous Polynesian populations, counted as parts of the USA and Chile, respectively).

It was my third visit to French Polynesia, and I spent some weeks visiting my old 'hunting grounds' from where I had Nice Memories: the capital Papeete, around the island of Tahiti by bus, and Tahiti's sister island Moorea with its Tiki Village Theatre. The latter is a kind of open museum with old style houses, artefacts, exhibitions and dance performances. The dances are a miracle of grace and beauty. Black pearls!

I took a flight to the atoll island of Rangiroa in the Tuamotu archipelago, where I had also been before. I longed to see something new, to travel even deeper into the country, to feel the suction of the Big Blue. But I had to give up the plans, because French Polynesia is so, so big, and the communications so, so sparse. I would have needed six months for French Polynesia alone.

Cook Islands

After French Polynesia I spent a few weeks in Cook Islands with the same purpose as in French Polynesia: to see my old 'haunts'. I thus saw the mini-capital Avarua, as well as Muri Beach, had an appointment with the famous naturopath and tour guide Pa, and saw more dances. The dances in Cook Islands are *even* more beautiful than those in French Polynesia. Then something new: Aitutaki, 'the world's most beautiful lagoon' according to the brochures. Yes, it qualifies. And at four o'clock in the morning the plane set off to New Zealand.

Auckland, New Zealand

After one month in Polynesia, I had, to say the least, a culture shock at my meeting with the metropolitan city of Auckland. High, high houses, many, many cars, hurry, hurry. Well, I would only stay there for two days waiting for the flight to Vanuatu, New Caledonia and Solomon Islands. Melanesia!

Solomon Islands – I was indeed hesitating as to whether I should go there. *Lonely Planet* and *BBC* had made me scared with reports of riots, curfews, criminality, foreign military presence, 'don't-travel-outside-the-capital', etc. Even the name Honiara sounded threatening. I would surely be robbed/raped/killed as soon as I put my nose outside the door. What was I getting into? Not only Solomon Islands; the whole of Melanesia seemed threatening – a lot of dos and don'ts: don't touch that plant, don't step over drains, don't go there if you are woman and...

A staff member, David, at the backpacker hostel in Auckland, was from Solomon Islands. He was happy to hear that I was going there and gave a lot of tips brochures and his mother's email address, and I thought that if people there were as nice as he, then it could not be that bad. I was beginning to look forward to Solomon Islands. But now Vanuatu was first in line.

The Pacific

Polynesia, Melanesia, Micronesia. The names flicker by. All three are parts of the Pacific Ocean, and all three are Greek words, which reveals that they are named by Europeans.

Polynesia – meaning 'many islands' – is situated in the eastern part of the Pacific Ocean and occupies the largest area, from Hawai'i in the north to New Zealand (or the indigenous name Aotearoa) in the south, from Tonga in the west to Easter Island (or Rapanui) in the east. It is one of the world's largest geographical areas, and there are indeed many islands. On the other hand, it is one of the most sparsely-populated, since most of its surface consists of water. In the east, the islands are atolls; in the west, they are volcanic islands, intensely green, with a mountain peak in the middle. Polynesia includes New Zealand/ Aotearoa, Cook Islands, French Polynesia (under France), Hawai'i (under USA), Niue, Easter Island/Rapanui (under Chile), Samoa, American Samoa (under USA), Tokelau (under New Zealand), Tonga, Tuvalu and Wallis-Futuna (under France).

Melanesia – 'black islands' – is situated in the south-west part of the Pacific, south of the equator, north-east of Australia and south-east of Papua New Guinea. The name Melanesia is controversial. Some scholars claim that it refers to the people, since they are much darker than in the rest of the Pacific. Another interpretation is that it is the islands that are black, not the people. The islands are high and mountainous, and from a distance they appear black against the horizon. Melanesia includes Fiji, New Caledonia (under France), Solomon Islands and Vanuatu, and sometimes Papua New Guinea.

Fiji has an exceptional position. Geographically Fiji is a country in Melanesia, and ethnically speaking the Fijians are Melanesians. On the other hand, culturally and historically, Fiji has much more in common with Polynesia. There are numerous legends and myths that tie Fiji to Samoa and Tonga.

Micronesia – 'small islands' – is situated north of Melanesia, just north of the equator and east of the Philippines. And most certainly they are small: small atolls which hardly stick their nose above the water surface. The bedrock consists of coral or limestone. The countries are: Federated States of Micronesia (sometimes simply 'Micronesia'), Guam (under USA), Kiribati, Marshall Islands, Nauru and Palau.

A Scent of Melanesia

Welkam to Vanuatu

Melanesia hit me like a fist in the stomach. Certainly a kind fist, but nevertheless a powerful one. Actually, I had no expectations in advance; still, I immediately felt on arrival that this would not be like anything else I had experienced so far. But I felt *welkam*, the word for 'welcome'.

When the plane dropped over the coconut plantations, I was terrified. Here I had *never* been before. The guidebook warnings as well as my own fear returned to my mind; 'the whole of Melanesia seemed threatening', etc. But the tension released when we landed at Bauerfield Airport in the capital Port Vila. In the arrival hall an amusing music group was performing, in blue flowery shirts, green flowery lavalavas and with wreaths of flowers on their head. They were playing string band, some kind of swinging Dixie, which I would forever after associate with Vanuatu.

'...walk a hundred meters to the exit where the main road leaves the airport parking lot and wait for a regular public bus'. Those were the instructions in *Lonely Planet*. I walked a hundred metres; a middle-aged woman with a little girl stopped a regular public bus and helped me 'on board'. The woman, sturdy, dark-skinned with afro-hair, was sun-shine all through, and the girl, with long, black hair, had the most de-lightful grace in her little face. This was my first meeting with Melanesians.

And there would be more meetings, for example at the conference at the Cultural Center in Port Vila (or Kaljoral Senta as it is written in Bislama, one of the three official languages in Vanuatu).

Cultural Center

The Cultural Center, a building built in a modern style, is located right opposite the Parliament. The conference had been arranged to gather ongoing research about Vanuatu. There were anthropologists, archaeo-logists, cultural workers, linguists, social scientists and gender re-searchers from all over the world, as well as from Vanuatu, of course. It is Vanuatu, together with Solomon Islands, that displays the largest cultural variation in the whole Pacific.

To my disappointment, most of the presentations were held in Bislama, which is quite different from English. And this in spite of the fact that the titles in the programme sheet were in English.

During the breaks they showed documentary films. One touching, almost poetic, film was about the searching for a song, and I began to understand in earnest that this was Melanesia, not Polynesia but something different, something deeper.

And I learnt something more. In Vanuatu, as well as in the rest of Melanesia, there are two parallel legal systems: the local *kastom* system and the colonial-inspired central administration. Minor conflicts are usually solved locally, while serious crimes are referred to central courts. Kastom (Eng. Custom, Fr. Coutume) is a generic term for everything deriving from the own traditional culture, before foreign influence.

The cement for Melanesian kastom is the *wantok* system, obligations to help somebody with the same language. Wantok means literally 'one-talk', that is 'same language'. Since Melanesia in general is characterized by an abundance of local languages, the language forms a kind of affinity. Somebody with the same language is almost a relative.

In addition to the conference room, the Cultural Center also includes a research library and a museum. The museum displays artefacts from all the islands of Vanuatu: canoes, baskets, spears, bark works, masks. Some masks and other cult artefacts radiate strong power and are eerie. Still, the 'strongest' artefacts, the 'magic stones', are locked up in the museum vault. These are artefacts you can use to harm other people.

The farewell party offered traditional dances by a troupe from Pentecost. The dances were striking; performed in the light from fire and solely with male dancers. Men in loincloths of grass and woven *pandanus* leaves and with rattling shell chains danced to drums as the sole instrument. The rhythm was hard and fiery. Sweaty backs shone in the lanterns. The dances were warlike, radiating power, not soft and erotic like the Polynesian ones, not intended to please but to frighten.

And it was needed. The whole Pacific has been the subject of European influence: 'discoverers', traders, missionaries and colonizers. To some extent, this contact brought a mutual exchange, but also – with or without intention – a great deal of damage. One example is the so-called blackbirding in the 19th century. Some 29,000 islanders from the whole Pacific, but mostly Melanesia, were recruited or kidnapped to go to Australia or Fiji to work in the sugar plantations.

This unprecedented contact with the wider world meant that the islanders also contracted its sicknesses and died like flies. By 1920, Vanuatu's population had dropped from 500,000 to only 40,000. The islanders resisted as much as they could, and warfare with head-hunting and cannibalism made Melanesia a dangerous part of the world.

Mele Maat

After the conference I wanted to learn a little more about the country and chose to stay in the village of Mele Maat in their small-scale model of tourism – Village Stay. Chief David and his wife welcomed me with dignity, humour and warmth. I was shown around and presented to *everyone* in the village, and it was quite a big village. I was put into a little cottage, made of leaves from the *sago* palm.

As a gift to Chief David, I had brought some *kava* roots. The crushed roots from the kava bush are mixed with water for drinking. It is commonly used in the Pacific, especially in Vanuatu, Fiji, Tonga and Samoa and gives a mild intoxication. Kava plays an important cultural role, and the preparation and drinking are ritualized.

In the afternoon there was a ceremony for three deaths, which had occurred one year earlier, with bible-reading and mild singing in Bislama. After this, I was invited to go with the villagers to the burial site and to place some flowers. At first, I felt the super-Swedish fear of imposing, but on the contrary, they were *honoured* by my presence and shared their flowers with me. It was an old man and two little twin girls who had died almost at the same time. We placed the flowers and stood by the graves for a while. The widow wept silently. The mother of the two little girls did not seem, in my eyes, very affected.

'It's all right,' she smiled.

Self-control is a virtue in Melanesia. Or the infant mortality is so high that nobody really counts their children under a certain age.

Then I walked around and studied the simple tombstones. Strikingly many had died young, at 40, 30, and yes, 20. The villagers told me that she or he had been perfectly well but one day just fell down and died, and they also knew why: sorcery, witchcraft.

Outside Mele Maat I visited The Secret Garden or Mele Cultural Centre and Nature Reserve – a botanical and cultural park. There were traditional houses and canoes, and everywhere I could see signs with information about the pre-Christian Vanuatu, about the history of Melanesia and Mele Maat and about the all-prevailing kastom system.

Vanuatu has a wild history with extensive cannibalism, of which the latest known case happened in 1969. Cannibalism has taken place in many parts of the world, for many reasons. One strong factor in the Pacific has been the need to get access to *mana*, spiritual power. Eating the enemy is the ultimate conquer. More base reasons like the need for protein cannot be excluded either, and in Vanuatu there are stories that the meat of 'long-pig' simply was *tasty*, tastier than pork. Therefore, they kept humans as, yes, cattle and commodities. To get over the psychological barrier to eat other fellow humans, they thus identified the victims as 'different', either slaves or enemies.

More tales and creepy legends. Blood, body parts, death. Finally, it just became too much. I had some kind of mental short-circuit from all the experiences. I felt that I could not take anymore. I could not be the monkey in the cage, I could not be the sensation of the village, and I thought that if there came one more person wanting to shake hands or one more child shouting 'hello', then I didn't know what I would do. I could not get angry with those sweet people. And all those questions: 'How many children do you have?' (Not: 'Do you have children?') 'Where is your husband?' (Not: 'Are you married?') Culturally bound questions that demanded culturally bound answers, which I could not give. You are not supposed to be single and childless.

Bonjour Nouvelle-Calédonie

The next Melanesian country in my travel plan was Nouvelle-Calédonie, or New Caledonia, a territory still under France. The capital Noumea is a kind of 'Little Paris'. It is a multi-cultural town. Here are Kanaks, i.e., the indigenous inhabitants, as well as French, Tahitians, Chinese, Vietnamese and Javanese. Surprisingly to me, there were many Polynesians. They even have their own shop, *Tahiti*. My roommate from the youth hostel confirmed that 10% of Noumea's population are from French Polynesia. They come there to work.

'It's so easy,' she said, 'same currency (i.e., XPF, Pacific-francs) and same language (that is French). And so close, only a five-hour flight.' That is exactly what she said: 'only a five-hour flight'. I, being from the small-scale Europe, have other definitions of 'close'...

After a few days in Noumea I took a speed boat to Ile des Pins, a smaller island where I stayed at the locally-owned accommodation Gîte Nataiwatch. I had rented a tent which I shared with Megan, a woman from Switzerland I met there.

Not far from Gîte Nataiwatch you can see Le Rocher or The Rock inside the water a few meters from the shore. There was something magic about it; the rock, as well as the water, changed colour according to the daylight. One afternoon I snorkelled around it. I found myself in an enormous school of fish, silvery, similar to herring, and suddenly I felt like I was inside a symphony. Millions of fish, over, under, before or behind me, the largest school I had ever seen, let alone swum inside. Suddenly, the school disappeared, and the corals were visible. Light blue-purple and turquoise branch corals shone towards me, as well as all kinds of fish you could ever imagine. But the water was cold.

The Rock was fascinating. Chiselled into the rock was a landing with two carved poles. It must be some sort of tourist decoration. Some rough steps led there; I would have to climb a little. But the landing was an altar, and I understood, *felt*, that this wasn't a tourist ploy. This wasn't for me. The sense of gravity made me turn and go back.

Later I read in a brochure that it is forbidden to climb the rock; it is sacred. Yet later I heard that a Japanese woman had been killed because she had climbed it. Some said that there were signs with warnings in French, but that she didn't know French. But I hadn't seen any signs. And yet later I heard from the local woman at the tourist information centre in the nearby town Vao, that the ancestral spirits live there. Yes, the carved poles, resembling the traditional Kanak rooftop spears, represent the ancestral spirits. That explains it. It also explains the sense of worship and magic I felt.

On the maps, the rock is only named Le Rocher or The Rock. I asked a man about its real name; he hesitated and then said that he had 'forgotten'. Too sacred to be even uttered perhaps, especially for strangers?

Back in Noumea, I took the bus to Centre Culturel Tjibaou. The centre is located outside Noumea, a futuristic building with three towers reminding me of giant corsets. It is named after the independence leader Jean Marie Tjibaou, who was assassinated in 1989, and includes art exhibitions, media displays and a botanic-cultural park. Along an arranged path named Chemin Kanak or Kanak Road, informative signs tell visitors about the plants, their names and their medical and cultural importance. The use of the coconut palm is endless. Trunk, leaves, nuts – everything is used in some way. Pandanus is not edible, but the leaves are used for mats and baskets. Croton, especially red, is a shrub which is planted in the whole of Pacific to mark land borders and graves.

From New Caledonia I returned to Vanuatu in order to change flights to Solomon Islands. The reunion with Vanuatu was warm, both temperature-wise and emotionally. The same string band played at the airport. Imagine, I arrived here six weeks ago – how unsure I felt, how little I knew, how new everything was. Now it was as if I had lived in Melanesia my whole life.

When checking in at Bauerfield Airport there were only five other passengers for Honiara, all Caucasians or 'Whites' as they are referred to in Melanesia. Hmm, is it so bad in Solomon Islands that nobody goes there? New riots? But I shouldn't have worried; half an hour before departure, all the Melanesian passengers poured forth, both from Vanuatu and from Solomon Islands. Of course. Only people from less relaxed parts of the world, come two hours before departure.

King Solomon's Hidden Treasure

A new country to love

The origin of the name Solomon Islands is obscured in layers of history. This group of islands was, according to legends, known among the Inca population in Peru already in the 16th century. The Spanish colonizers in Peru called them Islas Salomón, because they believed that it was the country where King Solomon's treasure was hidden. On that basis they convinced the Spanish King Philip II to pay for an expedition, led by Captain Don Álvaro de Mendaña de Neira. Mendaña thus 'discovered' the group of islands in 1568 for Europe. (That is, despite the country already having been discovered by the people who lived there, as well as by the Incas in Peru.) In English, the name became Solomon Islands.

A new country to love. How much I had feared it, and now after 14 years, this is my home country.

Solomon Islands shares history and culture to a large extent with Vanuatu. Here, too, people used to live in small ethnic groups on the islands, sometimes violently with head-hunting and cannibalism, and here, too, the society is built upon the traditional kastom and wantok systems. And here, too, came traders, blackbirders, missionaries and colonizers who would affect the future of the country forever.

According to *Lonely Planet*, I could take a bus from Henderson Airport to Honiara 'under the trees by the main road'. 'Under the trees by the main road,' I chanted to myself as I walked with my baggage. Look, a big road and look, trees and look, a minibus! The driver asked me with his eyebrows, as they do in Melanesia, if I wanted to go with his bus, and I confirmed, also with the eyebrows. But in what direction was Honiara? I could not ask lest I breach the Traveller's Rule 1A:

'When you arrive at a place for the first time, act as if you have been there hundreds of times before and know all rules and prices and don't intend to be cheated.'

I had a 50% chance to succeed... And in Honiara centre they dropped me at the little six-cornered green kiosk of the Visitors Bureau. There worked an Angel, who gave me maps, brochures, phoned Bulaia Lodge, which I had got tips about in Sweden, and *drove* me there! In that way I arrived at a cosy guest house with only local guests, a kaleidoscope of islanders. It is situated in Chinatown, a blue two-storey building with the cheerful sign Bulaia Backpacker Lodge. But I never saw any backpackers. An airy sitting-room with high ceilings and a little kitchen. I got a bed in a dorm for four, all by myself. 'Dorm' is called 'transit room' here.

The receptionist Shirley showed me 'the burnt city', the ruins after the burnt Chinese stores from the riots five months earlier. This now made up my view. Distorted iron skeletons still poked up from the rich green of tropical plants, which had taken over the grounds of the buildings. Bulaia Lodge, too, had been seriously threatened by the fire. The riots were aimed at the Chinese-owned stores, and Bulaia Lodge is Solomon-owned, but what does fire care about nationalities?

I lay on the bed, while the sun was setting and the cicadas were bellowing. In the evening it was a bit noisy outside, and some guests were obviously drinking. Maybe not the best place after all? It could be cleaner. But anyway, I had reached my goal. *Zzzz...*

Solomon Islands in short

After Captain Mendaña's visit in 1568, it was another 200 years (called 'The Great Peace' by the islanders) until European conquerors and missionaries began the colonization. Solomon Islands, too, was affected by the blackbirding. In the 1890s the country was established as a British protectorate. During World War II, Solomon Islands was the site for severe battles between Japan and the Allied forces.

Solomon Islands gained independence in 1978, but the country has remained as a member of the Commonwealth, with Queen Elizabeth II of England as Head of State. The regime is parliamentarian. Several internal disturbances have shaken the country. The ethnic tensions in 1998-2003, mostly between Guadalcanalians and Malaitans, were in practice a civil war with a death toll of several hundred. It was mostly Malaitans living in Guadalcanal who were killed. Even today, Malaitans won't dare to go into the inner areas of Guadalcanal.

These ethnic tensions led to the establishment of Regional Assistance Mission to Solomon Islands (RAMSI) in 2003, an Australian-led peacekeeping mission consisting of 15 countries to secure the country's stability. The fighting ceased the same year, but RAMSI stayed until 2018. RAMSI's role was controversial. For example, there were participants from Fiji (which recently had had a coup d'état), from Tonga (which recently had had riots) and Papua New Guinea (which had severe criminality). A drunk RAMSI-soldier on leave in New Caledonia shot and killed a woman. Two drunk drivers ran over and killed people on the road in Malaita. Talk about sweep your own floor first.

Most islanders live off agriculture and fishing. The most important raw materials are timber and fish but also *copra* (dried meat of coconut), palm oil, gold and minerals. Tourism is marginal. The country is situated in the 'Ring of Fire' (i.e., the countries surrounding the Pacific Ocean) with innumerable volcanic eruptions and earthquakes, but the country is largely spared from major cyclones. The climate is tropical.

Solomon Islands consists of six larger islands and c. 900 smaller ones. There are nine provinces: Central Province, Choiseul, Guadalcanal (or 'Guale' or 'Galekana'), Isabel, Makira, Malaita, Rennell & Bellona (or 'Renbel'), Temotu and Western Province. Understanding the geography is complicated by the fact that the old Spanish and English names are mixed with the local ones. For example, the Spanish-named island and province of 'San Cristobal' is nowadays referred to as 'Makira'. Maps and guide books are inconsistent; some use the Spanish name, some the English and some the local. Guadalcanal is named by a member of Captain Mendaña's crew after his village in Spain (which in its turn might have been named by the Arab conquerors)!

The nation has in 2020 c. 690,000 inhabitants, of which c. 90,000 live in Honiara.

The capital Honiara

Honiara was recently 'crowned' the dirtiest capital in the whole Pacific. Hm, well maybe. But they didn't say anything about the humblest taxi-drivers and the most honest market vendors. And the most wonderful people in the Pacific – yes, in the whole world.

Slowly I walked across the old bridge over the Mataniko River towards the city centre, smiling and being smiled at in return. The road was, and is, shaded by large flame trees. The main street, or actually *the* street, wears the elegant name Mendana Avenue and stretches along the coast, parallel with the harbour.

The town's marketplace, Honiara Central Market, was larger than the market in Port Vila, and in addition to vegetables, they also had a section for handicraft. No haggling over prices, always the correct change. Beside the fish market, some children were swimming at the pier. Outside the market I met a couple from the Vanuatu flight, who would sail and dive in Solomon Islands. They complained about the heat and that there were 'so many people'. Yes, it was quite crowded. They seriously thought that the main industry in this country was *tourism*. Ha-ha-ha. Instead, it is agriculture and fishing with simple tools, a fishtinning industry, a brewery with the tasty beer Solbrew and foreign logging companies. The country had in 2006 c. 11,500 visitors (in 2019 c. 27,900), compared to Fiji's annual almost 900,000 visitors.

I had planned to look around in Solomon Islands, and therefore I raced around like a scalded cat between Solomon Airlines in the town centre and the speed boat company *Solomon Express* east of town. This was four days before Christmas; it was like trying to get a train ticket in Sweden during the same time. Everything was full, and travel was seemingly impossible, but at last I stepped out from *Solomon Express'* office with my gems in my hand: boat tickets to Auki in Malaita over Christmas and to Gizo in Western Province (both provincial capitals) after New Year.

In the park at the Art Gallery there was an arts festival going on. Both the wood carvings and the contemporary paintings had motifs from traditional life and mythology. The artists told me how important it was to depict the old culture in new ways. The government supports this art in the form of public decoration. Banks, the telecommunications company Our Telekom, the post office and other institutions have their walls covered with paintings with mythological motifs, as well as the lamp posts and the big flower pots along Mendana Avenue.

Photo 1 (see end of book)

In the countless Chinese stores I discovered more and more what a crazy-cheap country this was. That is to say, for me. A fourth or fifth of the prices I had experienced in Vanuatu and New Caledonia. But with the buying power of the Solomon Islanders income, it was expensive. The currency is Solomon Islands Dollar, SBD (hereafter $ or dollar(s)). This was 2006. Now, 14 years later, currency rates and prices are surprisingly stable. Certain prices, mostly for goods and service for foreign visitors (beer, handicraft, hotel rooms and more) have risen dramatically. Yet other prices, e.g., for basic goods (rice, sugar) and home technology (mobiles, SIM-cards) are stable or slightly lower.

Back to 2006. I had not eaten anything for the whole day. It was half past four, and everything was closing. But in a simple lunch spot, a *kai*-bar (*kai* or *kaikai* = food), I bought fish and chips in a brown paper bag. The fish – tuna – was tasty, as were the chips of *kumara*, sweet potato. I went back to Bulaia Lodge. The TV in the sitting room showed mostly Australian programs but also Solomon Islands' own, by then, 'One News'. The water was off, but the staff brought buckets of water for a shower. I talked to the other guests. There was a group from Russell Islands in Central Province, who were in Honiara to negotiate with a

CURRENCY RATES
Approximate currency rates for Solomon Dollar (SBD)
October 2020

1 AUD = 5.82 SBD	1 SBD = 0.18 AUD
1 EUR = 9.61 SBD	1 SBD = 0.11 EUR
1 GBP = 10.55 SBD	1 SBD = 0.097 GBP
1 NZD = 5.35 SBD	1 SBD = 0.19 NZD
1 SEK = 0.92 SBD	1 SBD = 1.06 SEK
1 USD = 8.17 SBD	1 SBD = 0.12 USD

PRICE EXAMPLES 1, 2020, SBD

Rice 1 kg $10	Bus within town $3
Sugar 1 kg $10	Taxi $10/km
Simple lunch $35	Internet café $6/15 min
Fancy dinner $200	Internet mobile $6/24 tim
Beer in a bar $20	Simple hotel room/dorm $200

foreign logging company. Timber is one of the most important raw materials here, and logging is a giant industry with serious ecological impacts. The newspapers write about how the foreign loggers abuse teenage girls. It is mainly Asian companies that are involved.

The next day I continued my exploration of Honiara. Yes, the town was definitely filthy. The pavements were filled with paper, cartons, plastic bags, plastic bottles and coconut shells as well as with gobs of red spit. The spit comes from betel nut chewing. Women, men, old, young chew betel nut. You bite off the skin and put the nut in your mouth, dip a leaf in lime powder and chew it all together. And then spit where you happen to be. The mixture gives a mild intoxication, called 'Solomon Beer', and it colours the saliva red and eventually also the teeth. A Melanesian tale goes like this:

Betel Nut, Leaf and Lime
Once upon a time, there were Betel nut, Leaf and Lime. All three were friends, but they were living by themselves. Betel nut stayed in the Forest, Leaf grew on the Shore and Lime came from powdered coral in the Sea. Once, when the three came together they started a row, which led to a war. They were killing each other, and the ground was coloured red from their blood. We can see this red colour even today, when we mix Betel nut, Leaf and Lime. It will remind us to be friends and stay in peace with each other.

Betel nut chewing spreads tuberculosis, causes mouth cancer and is a nuisance. Many house walls have signs in Solomon Pijin, forbidding chewing and spitting:

NO BITOLNAT. IU SPIT IU KLIN
'NO BETEL NUT. YOU SPIT, YOU CLEAN'

But when you look up from the pavement of Mendana Avenue with the red spit and the shabby stores, you'll see the mighty crowns of the flame trees.

Photo 2

The heat was oppressive. I crossed the road right at Point Cruz, the town's very centre, at its crossroad between Mendana Avenue and Commonwealth Street and its insane traffic. Right there in the most dangerous spot, I jumped up on the pavement with an inch to spare and somehow still alive.

I looked up and saw something flicker in the heat. An emblem with SVERIGES KONSULAT. And another emblem with BUNDES-REPUBLIK DEUTSCHLAND HONORARKONSUL. Was I delirious...? No, it was real. Sweden's and Germany's consulates, my, my. Solomon Islands had representatives from only a few countries, and Sweden and Germany were apparently two of them. Why? was the question. I just had to find out, so I stepped in and had a chat with the consul Mr Gerald Stenzel. He looked a little worried when I stepped in, but I told him that I didn't have any problems, no stolen passport or such. No, this commitment as a consul, which he combined with trading, was really not very burdensome. I have kept in contact with the nice consul through the years with minor errands.

The pleasant shopping centre NPF Plaza has beautiful decorations on their friezes and wooden pillars with traditional designs. At that time, in 2006, they had some small stalls with simple lunch plates with local food. I ordered *taro* leaves baked in coconut milk and the delicious *ngali* nuts, which I ate sitting on a blue bench, at the same time enjoying the colourful wall paintings.

Just alongside the NPF Plaza, you can find the humble little National Museum. The museum's only room contains a three-dimensional papier mâché map of Solomon Islands, numerous photos, tools, costumes, models of canoes and more. There is also a museum shop. Its head, an enthusiastic woman named Patricia, is very helpful and happy that somebody wants to listen to her knowledge.

In 2006, in the yard outside the museum, you could admire wood carvings and houses from the various provinces, with walls and roof made of sago palm leaves. Even farther down the street is the post office and an internet café. Stamps and internet are cheap, too. But surely *something* has to be expensive!?

King Solomon Hotel is a luxury hotel at Hibiscus Avenue, parallel to Mendana Avenue, with beautiful interior decor and furniture in bamboo. On Tuesdays and Thursdays there are dance performances, and this, my second day of arrival, was a Thursday! Of course, I must attend it!

We were treated to the national music of Solomon Islands: *panpipes*, this evening from Malaita, performed by men in pale yellow grass skirts. Panpipes are built of bamboo canes of different size. The canes are tied in a row, from the longest to the shortest, which thus gives different resonance. The largest, up to one meter long, give a muffled hollow tone, while the smallest ones give a high-pitched flute tone. You can either blow them or beat them with a coconut husk or a rubber flip-flop. The instruments are heavy. As the men dance and swing them rhythmically, they droop from the weight. Around their left foot they have bands of shells, which rattle as they stamp. Beautiful and melancholic.

But the interesting feature was that *it sounded a little like the music of Peru*. A possible support of Thor Heyerdahl's hypothesis? As an addition to the generally accepted theory that the early migration to the Pacific took place from Asia and eastwards, Heyerdahl suggested ideas about a supplementary migration in the opposite direction, from South America and westwards. Through his Kon-Tiki voyage he demonstrated practically that it was *possible*. And the music, the music...? *And how could the Incas in Peru know about these islands???*

Photo 3

The next day, 22nd December and my birthday, the library was closed, as well as the museum, the post office and the internet café. What? It was certainly near Christmas but just an ordinary Friday. However, the Chinese stores were open, and the bustling trade could make any shopping centre in the world green with envy. Even if islanders don't exchange Christmas gifts here, they send goods to their families on the remote islands.

The stores were overcrowded, the air was smelly and choking. I saw a pair of flip-flops, but there wasn't even room enough to bend and try them on. But they cost only $5 so I took a chance. In the streets, people were moving in compact streams; a woman had fainted in the frying heat. Fragments of Jingle Bells were floating in the air.

I myself felt a strong sense of well-being. I was walking leisurely in the human tide, enjoying the beautiful calm Melanesian faces without any trace of Christmas stress. My blood ran easier. How would I manage the return to Sweden?

At the market I bought presents for myself: bracelets and necklaces made of Malaita's traditional shell works or *shell money*. I had a nice lunch in the Chinese restaurant Golden Crown, and in the octagon pavilion named Amy's, at the corner of Mendana Avenue and Commonwealth Street, I bought a piece of pineapple pie.

My birthday was successful. At Bulaia I was watching TV and talked with the other guests. Everyone was carrying babies, and I ended up doing that, too. The babies and toddlers go from arms to arms, women and men are lugging and cuddling. A family with three children had a little sick boy who cried for hours and hours.

The disco at Honiara Hotel across the street provided ear-splitting music until dawn.

Towards Malaita!

Malaita is only the second largest island in Solomon Islands after Guadalcanal, but it is the most populous. The Malaitans are proud and independent and on the whole known to be 'troublemakers', both towards earlier colonizers and missionaries and towards the present central government. Malaita has three main ethnic groups: *Kwara'ae* in the north, *Kwaio* in the middle and *'Are'are* in the south, with a number of smaller groups, e.g., *Langa Langa* and *Lau*. In the 19th century, head-hunting and cannibalism were practised among the ethnic groups themselves as well as towards those foreign visitors who dared to get there. And according to *Lonely Planet Solomon Islands* (1997), 'the most fierce, traditional and independent of the islanders' were the Kwaio. I wanted to try some kind of Village Stay in East Kwaio, a remote region on Malaita's east coast. But how could I get there?

Even if one does not travel in groups, in order to visit the inner part of East Kwaio, it is absolutely essential to have a local guide. Government officials discourage individual visits, and an early *Lonely Planet Solomon Islands* (1997) was not exactly encouraging:

Visits to the Kwaio

East-central Malaita Island's mountainous interior is only very seldom visited by Westerners, and you should think very carefully before going there. As government officials themselves require escorts here, they discourage foreigners from contacting the Kwaio. Nonetheless, trips inland are possible for those who can afford to pay penalty rates for guides, and are prepared for the possibility of an angry, perhaps even violent, rejection by the Kwaio once they find them. The Kwaio may also demand huge compensation.

But with time, there has been some establishment of the tourist visits, and a later *Lonely Planet Solomon Islands* (2008) took a different tone:

Ready for a culture shock? Consider visiting the traditional 'bush' Kwaio, who live in eastern-central Malaita's mountainous interior. [...] This is not your average 'cultural experience': you do have to come prepared to avoid cultural faux pas with potentially serious consequences.

We met Ronnie Butala, a 'modern Kwaio' [...] who can organize two- to three-day guided trips to meet the bush Kwaio.

One thing is sure: a visit to the Kwaio is a life-altering experience. [...] Wanna question your own way of life? Contact Ronnie Butala...

So I contacted Ronnie Butala. I already had his name via the Swedish travel agency *Läs & Res* [Read & Travel] – one of the few travel agencies in the world that used to arrange group travelling to East Kwaio. Ronnie was accustomed to Swedish visitors. I told him that I wanted to try some kind of Village Stay in East Kwaio. The sum he mentioned for car and boat rental made me lose my breath! And now my phone card was empty, after two domestic calls! Now I knew what was expensive here: phone calls and transport in the form of petrol.

But I accepted his plan. Ronnie lived in Auki, and since I already had a boat ticket to Auki for the next day, we agreed that he would meet me there.

Next morning the nice staff in the harbour office let me put my baggage in there, while I did the last shopping: among other things, candies and balloons for the children and a tray of beer that Ronnie asked me to buy. Alcohol is only sold in special Bottle Shops, and I found one in the harbour. The sales staff and the precious goods are protected with iron bars. The beer was heavy, and then I had three more bags. Even today I don't know how I managed.

By the piers, I saw some decrepit looking cargo-passenger ships who slowly but surely were filled with cargo and passengers. Some were already crammed-full. I watched them with discomfort and was glad I would go by speed boat. At the same time, I enjoyed the dynamism in the harbour; people were crowding, loading baggage, being busy. When I had found the *Solomon Express*, I fetched my baggage from the harbour office in two rounds. I asked some co-passengers to look after it and thought that either the bags would be stolen, or the beer. But no.

When the speed boat arrived, there was a sudden incredible chaos. Queues don't exist. Unlike the cargo-passenger ships, which will take as many passengers as possible, the speed boat takes only as many as have numbered tickets. In spite of this, everyone tried to get on board at the same time, hysterical that they would be left behind. There was no gangway; we had to step over the rail, and try to do that with three bags and a tray of beer. One woman forced her adult children to help me, which they did, but only until we were on board, not further. All passengers with seats 1-50 went *downstairs*, before they discovered that they should have gone *upstairs*. But they could not go back, since the passengers with seats 51-200 were pushing behind them. The crew tried to direct with megaphones. Still, the speed boat was not full. There were some empty seats, for example beside me, lucky me, and I forced down my bags. Still I was folded like a pocket-knife. Around me children were screaming, crawling, climbing, shooting with flashing plastic guns, shaking and kicking my seat. I rebuked them, mildly, but felt like Angry White Missis. It was not a pleasant voyage.

The speed boat tied up at Auki. In the harbour, villagers were paddling quietly in dugout canoes against the background of Lilisiana village with leaf houses and palms. The little harbour town of Auki was something totally different from Honiara. A calm. I was met by Ronnie, who told me that a car would come and pick us up for further transport across the island. Crowds of people were sitting or lying on the ground since last night, waiting for trucks to take them to various parts of the island.

Everything was delayed; for example, we did not find petrol. At last Ronnie suggested that we should stay with him and go early the next morning. He and his wife Elsie had a modern villa on a hill. Modern yes, but since the running water was off, the alternative was a bucket of water and a scoop in the basement. The only restaurant in Auki was closed for Christmas. Instead, we strolled along the harbour and bought grilled fish and pineapple. The sunset at the harbour was incredible; the sky was, *I promise*, bright pink towards orange behind the black coconut palms.

Christmas in Gounabusu

The next day, Christmas Eve, we set off. But a private car is not the best vehicle to get across the mountainous and rough road, the only road across the island that exists. Soon, the engine began to boil, and the driver had to go to a village and ask for help. He returned with a kettle of water, together with all the children in the village. The car and I were the Event of the Day. The driver fiddled with the engine for half an hour without result, and at last we got a lift with a private pickup until we reached Malaita's east coast.

There, in the little harbour of Atori, we continued in a motorboat, OBM or 'engine canoe' as they call it here. Outside the reef the sea was rough, and the boat was pitching. Hard. I hit my butt on the sitting board and continued to feel pain even after three days. After two hours we arrived at the beautiful bay of Sinaragu. In Gounabusu we stepped ashore, took our belongings, and I was installed in Ronnie's father's house on a mattress on the floor.

The friendly village of Gounabusu is located on a small strip of shore deep inside Sinaragu bay. Over us rise the mighty mountains, covered by a deep rainforest, frightening and attracting. The village is large and has both a primary school, a secondary school, a little clinic and a football field, cut out from the forest. It has a station for shortwave radio, at that time the only communication with the surrounding world. Here there were, in addition to the traditional palm leaf houses, so-called permanent houses of wood. My host family had a permanent house, freshly painted in a pale blue colour with white window frames. Outside, a bright red parrot was chained to a line.

As a water source the village had some ten taps, also used for personal hygiene. They were open, and you just had to perform the feat of having a shower *inside* a lavalava. It is important for a woman to cover her body between the waist and the knees, but there are no problems with showering topless or, by all means, breastfeeding in public. (Women's breasts don't mean *sex* here but *baby food*.) Toilet business was handled on a ledge a short way up a path. Thus crouching, you had an excellent view over the village.

After the relative anonymity in Honiara, this was my first personal contact with the Solomon Islanders. During a stroll through the village, I was introduced to everyone and was received with a friendly manner. But unlike Mele Maat in Vanuatu, persons were a little more reserved; they were not quite that open and welcoming but neither that curious. Ronnie was an excellent guide; he was telling and showing and knew what tourists want to do. They want, for example, to try local activities like grating mangrove fruits or coconuts and to be photographed doing that. Like me.

In the evening, villagers gathered at my host family, the only one with electric light – from solar cells on the roof. I was sitting on the stairs to the separate kitchen (all rural kitchens are separate huts.), together with some women who treated me with the latest gossip; it was quite delicate.

Outside the church a female choir was performing: gospel combined with homemade rhythmic instruments and traditional dances. The skilful and touching little troop was preparing to go to a festival in Honiara.

Most of them had never been outside the village and were full of anticipation.

On Christmas morning I was awakened by a baby crying. What? In this house there were no babies. I went outside to have a look. It was the family with three children from Honiara – oh no, not that little screamer again. He was still screaming, hysterically. The family had arrived at half past four in the morning and was having a rest in Ronnie's father's house. They were overloaded with baggage, which they left to collect later. They had yet another two hours to go on jungle paths up into the mountains. Thus (I counted): 7 hours on a cargo-passenger ship from Honiara, 4 hours in truck from Auki, 2 hours with motorboat from Atori, 2 hours' walk on jungle paths. With three children under three years of age and baggage: 4 rice sacks at 10 kg, 4 suitcases, 3 smaller bags, 2 cartons, 1 woven mat and 1 mattress. And I complained about my own little effort!

The inhabitants in Gounabusu and in the other villages, situated as a pearl necklace along the coast, are 'coastal Kwaio'. Up in the mountains live the 'bush Kwaio' or the 'hidden people' as they are referred to among the Kwaio themselves. They live according to their indigenous traditions. The two Kwaio groups have close contacts, often with kinship bonds.

The hidden people are reserved towards strangers. In the 'good old times', visitors could come to harm or simply disappear and never be found. But if the contact is done properly, with a local guide they trust, they welcome small organised tours. And they know about Sweden from Ronnie. Swedes, who have been the most common nationality, are considered generally more respectful than other nationalities. When they are told not to take photos, they obey. They are thus the most popular nationality. That was nice for me to hear.

Now, should I go with Ronnie to the hidden people? But the night before there was a heavy rain, and the steep muddy paths made it impossible. So that expedition we could forget. Instead, we did shorter tours along the coast with the motorboat. People and goods were to be moved from one village to another. For example, they moved a sawmill. The five-meter-long saw was lid on the rails with exact balance, so the boat would not tip.

On the big field the children were playing football. A man complained to me that children nowadays otherwise don't play; they just watch video violence and become violent themselves. I said the problem was the same in Sweden. But video, here? Oh yes, one family had a private generator, a video player and a TV screen. All you need!

A woman in Gounabusu was married to a Polynesian man from Rennell Island. With his fair skin and smooth black hair, compared to Kwaio's medium-brown skin and reddish-brown, even blond, frizzy hair, he was just as exotic as I. Another outsider was a woman from Shortland Island. Her almost black skin and long shiny black hair aroused attention, too. We laughed and called ourselves 'the three foreigners'. They meant *seriously* that they were just as foreign as I, no matter they were Solomon Islanders and spoke Pijin. But not Kwaio. And were the wrong colour.

Ronnie showed me the burial site, up a path, where his mother was buried. It was a sarcophagus-like grave with a roof, surrounded by that red croton I remembered from New Caledonia (and also from Samoa). The other graves were simpler. Not one had any name; everyone knew anyway who lay where. Some were decorated with plastic flowers. An old respected man was buried here the year before. The hidden people considered that his skull should be kept with them in their skull house, but this was rejected by the Christian coastal Kwaio. Then one night, half a year after the death, some men came down from the mountains, dug out what was left of the body, took his head and returned quietly with it to the mountains.

A path and a mangrove swamp led to the next village. There sat an old woman with beautiful geometric facial tattoos. She had had them done as a young girl among the hidden people. Now she had converted to Christianity and felt ashamed of her tattoos; did not want me to take a photo. But with a mischievous smile she took a stick and put it quickly through her nose wall and had a good laugh at my surprise. She had made a hole through her nose wall at the same time as the tattoos. And she showed me her most precious property: a traditional pendant, *la'uniasi*, a round white plate made of a clam shell, with black engraving.

Many older villagers, both men and women, have facial tattoos with geometrical designs, and I have my Samoan arm tattoos, so we compared designs and techniques. And in Langa Langa, many people have coil-shaped burn-scars on their cheeks, even youngsters.

We returned to Gounabusu paddling a dugout canoe through the mangrove swamp, quiet with the waves lapping around the bow; I enjoyed it deeply. There was dinner at Ronnie's father's house. A pig had been slaughtered, baked in a *motu* and shared between the villagers.

A motu is a temporary oven built of stones. Firewood is stacked and, on top of that, stones. The wood is set on fire, and when it has burnt down, the stones are hot. The food which is to be baked is wrapped in banana leaves and placed together with the stones. Everything is covered with more banana leaves and/or empty sacks, and then there is nothing more to do but wait, hungry. It is a common way of cooking all over the Pacific. But unlike a Solomon motu, which is built up on the ground, an earth oven in the rest of the Pacific, *umu*, is dug as a hole down in the ground. But regardless of up or down, this method is unbeatable when it comes to keeping the natural moistness and flavour of the food.

Photo 4

At this Christmas in Gounabusu, there were beer, but it was consumed very discreetly. Drinking is a big problem in Solomon Islands, and Gounabusu has taken a strong stand against it. With a fine of $50 the following are forbidden in the village: alcohol consumption, selling marijuana or tobacco, swearing, causing fighting, gambling about money, Sunday marketing, weapon assaulting, trousers on women and other misconduct...

I was sitting at the beach while the darkness lowered, listening to the choir rehearsing before the trip to Honiara. Fire flies were shining. Small talk. When I stood up with my torch, a little troop of children shouted,

'Torch!'

They stood up as one person and followed me like a little quiet tail. In my European narrow-mindedness I thought they wanted to join someone with a torch, especially across the troublesome drain, but no. When we reached the drain, they turned and went back in darkness. They just wanted to escort me.

'Our culture,' said Ronnie.

Curious sounds at night. A woman was singing a sad little song with a thin voice. And a dog was howling in a way I had never heard a dog howl before. Or wasn't it a dog? Sometimes I wonder how much I was awake and how much I was dreaming.

Dolphin Center and Kwai Island

There was time to leave Gounabusu. Ronnie would take me back to Auki, and we stepped into the motorboat. There was a strong wind. We approached the first reef, the driver waited for a suitable wave, and a woman with a hen in her arms shouted,

'Hold strong!'

And that was needed; the little boat pitched in the rough swells outside the reef, and we were thrown around like corks. The engine stopped twice, leaving us bobbing helplessly. I saw in my mind's eye the newspaper headline: 'Swedish woman drowned in Solomon Islands'. These waters are known to be difficult; the reefs cross each other here and there. Finally, after an hour we arrived at Solomon Dolphin Center. This establishment is sometimes used by Japanese dolphin researchers, but otherwise it is free for rental. It is run by a nice elderly couple and consists of a jetty out in the water with guest rooms, all in wood. When we arrived, some canoes were bobbing outside. The man wanted me to take photos of the centre and advertise it. He was very well read and asked me to send him a book about 'Political Science' when I was back overseas, which I did.

Opposite the centre is the small island of Kwai, and although a strong wind still blew, the woman paddled me there. It is a peculiar island, artificial in the sense that the villagers have raised the ground over the sea level with the help of dead coral, stone and sand, and planted bushes and coconut palms. It is seldom possible to grow anything else on such artificial islands, or to get water except via rainwater tanks. The villagers live off fish and crops on the main island. During droughts they collect water from the main island or drink coconuts. On Kwai, the houses are squeezed tightly and regularly, like a town. One joker had painted 'King's Road' on a wall. There are 1,000 inhabitants on the island, which you can walk around in 20 minutes. It teems with children who in 10-20 years will be ready for marriage. How will this end?

Back at the Dolphin Center, the woman asked shyly if I could pay 100 dollars for bed, food and paddling. I could. It was so peaceful there on their jetty. I would have liked to stay one more day and relax, but we had agreed about transport back to Auki the next morning. Darkness fell; we were chatting and relaxing on the jetty in the velvet night.

We were to get up at two o'clock – ouch. I woke Ronnie, who mumbled that we were going at three instead. Now, as I was awake, I went outside and stood there stunned. A sun- and moon-bridge I have seen. But this was a *star*-bridge. All the sky's stars were shining strongly, and in the black water they made up a glittering highway to our Dolphin Center. On the Three Sisters Islands out in the sea, some lighthouses were twinkling. I came to think of Georg I. Hindersson's book *Pala Pala* (2005):

At around 10 o'clock last night he was leaning over the starboard ramp looking dreamily out into the dark night sky. The moon had not yet risen and he saw only the sparkling celestial dome arched over his head, so close that he felt he might reach out and touch it. In this pitch-black dome, the dazzling stars were like holes. Tiny peepholes leading to beautiful fantasies on the other side. Yes, as usual, the return of the crystal-clear air brought sacred experiences.

Freely translated from Swedish by Jean Hudson

Then Hindersson continues in the same poetic, mystic way to describe the maritime phenomenon *Te lapa*, flashes and lights under the water. Known to navigators through the millennia, still scientifically unexplained. Earth magnetic tensions? Reflexes, but from what?

Three o'clock then, a lighthouse keeper drove us the last distance to Atori, where the crammed-full truck was waiting to take us back to Auki. Ronnie had booked seats in the front. Usually I avoid luxury treatments like that, but now I was actually grateful. First, we were chatting vividly, but then sleep took over. My head was jerking to and fro. Over and over, it was drawn to Ronnie's warm and soft shoulder instead of the cold hard car door, and I flinched, embarrassed. The truck breathed heavily for three hours on bad roads, and just before Auki we saw the sunrise. All the passengers were let off in the harbour.

Auki

Ronnie and his wife had their house full of relatives, and since I did not want to be a burden to them, I checked in at Auki Motel. This was probably the neatest and cleanest place I had seen in Solomon Islands; the slightest tap was working – strange. The room had a mirror, and for the first time for three months I saw myself in full figure. I could hardly recognize myself. How thin I was! My clothes hung around me. After the meagre meals and my lifestyle, where I was constantly in motion, I had probably lost 10 kg. In two months.

Among the guests were a Swiss physician couple, who were working at National Referral Hospital in Honiara. We talked for a long time. After having seen incongruities at the hospital they had a critical, very European attitude to Solomon Islands. In their frustration, they had shouted at the nurses. I did not doubt the incongruities, but the solution, the solution.

'You have to put yourself in a position of respect,' they said. But it cannot be done like that. You cannot master Melanesians. *It can only have the opposite effect.* And it had.

In the street, a troop of heavily armed Australian RAMSI-soldiers were passing by and waved comradely to us. Many Solomon Islanders still felt uncomfortable to see foreign machine guns in their own country.

I joined the Swiss and their guide Silas for half an hour's walk through the greenery to the Lilisiana village with its lovely sand beach. We were snorkelling, and I saw a kind of finger corals I hadn't seen before: white with black tips and much bigger than the common finger corals.

Silas told us that he had recorded unique traditional music, lullabies and others, mixed with modern music, and he wanted to make a CD. He played a lovely lullaby for us.

In the evening I enjoyed the coolness on the veranda at Auki Motel. The day had been unbelievably hot and humid, and now my body smelled of fresh yoghurt again. It happens when you have just had a shower and the sweat is rushing out before the skin has even become dirty. It is not unpleasant, it just indicates how hot it is.

At the same time, just as in Mele Maat in Vanuatu, I felt tired. Living as the only foreigner in traditional villages brings dizzying cultural experiences. I adapt easily and assimilate to the villagers' way of living. But the isolation from the big world and the intensity takes its toll. Now it felt as if Melanesia was devouring me. I was pulled into a dark mystic, blood cult with magic stones, head-hunting. There were so many things I would like to convey; I would like to open a Melanesian travel agency, or a cultural centre, or...

At least I have been able to write this book.

Back to Honiara

It was time to return to Honiara. I strolled in Auki, which I had become so fond of. In the harbour I saw the two large cargo-passenger ships *Tomoko* (= war canoe) and *Temotu*. Fascinated, I was pulled irresistibly there and followed the labour-intensive process of loading baggage and passengers. Now the sacks were filled with kumara and other root crops to be brought back to Honiara. Pineapples in bunches were hauled from the market to be sold in Honiara. The best pineapple in Solomon Islands comes from Malaita, and this was the season. The whole crew shouted or used megaphones, layered with the salvation tunes from a pastor.

And they say that Melanesians cannot plan and organise. But the country would not work without those everyday heroes, who lift and carry and fix to make their relatives in the villages on the remote islands have an acceptable life. At the same time, the people in town supplement their meagre budget with free food from their land. The land means everything here; it gives continuity and identity and provides a warranty for future generations. In the same way I understand the large number of children. Having many children does not only mean a secured old age. The children fill a function already now. More children do not only mean more mouths to feed – there is free food in abundance – but also more hands to lift and carry, more youth to move to Honiara and bring home more goods.

The sun was shining over the quay, and the smell was compact from human sweat, mud and rotten fruit. The *Temotu* offered a merciful shade for everyone who was just standing there watching, or waiting for the next ship, like me.

The next ship – oh yes, it will arrive soon, and here I stand dreaming! I hurried to Auki Motel and picked up my baggage. But have you, reader, ever hurried in flip-flops on a mud street? Exactly, the mud splashes up on your backside and makes a splattered pattern. If you walk barefoot, this will not happen.

And have you ever seen a Solomon ship arrive on time? *Solomon Express* was delayed again; I should have known that. So there was really no need to rush.

Then there was the same chaos as before; the entering passengers pushed and squeezed off the leaving passengers. A crew member used a megaphone to direct the crowds. Ragged and tousled, everyone found their seats, and then began the big *freezing*. The air-conditioning was set at 22°C, ice, and the passengers put on long-sleeved shirts and jackets. My fingertips slowly went numb during the three-hour long voyage. The woman beside me asked if it was cold in Sweden.

'Like here,' I answered, 'when it is at its warmest.'

She flinched. You may think that 22°C is not very cold, but since people here – and I – are used to living day and night in a woolly 32°C blanket, then...

A screen was showing comic slapsticks from Nigeria. I had never seen any Nigerian film productions before, and now I did it here in Solomon Islands. We screamed with laughter at the funny episodes. Later, the crew came and warned about currents and distributed seasick-bags just in case, but nothing happened. At three we arrived in Honiara. *Temotu* was already anchored there. I mean, *Solomon Express* was twice as expensive because it was supposed to be twice as fast, and then *Temotu* was faster anyway.

Happy New Year!

Honiara! My fingertips were still numb when I walked up to the neat United Church Rest House. I had seen that rest house from the outside and wanted to try it. I took a transit bed on the ground floor. Upstairs they have the spacious dining room, and from the veranda I saw the port of Honiara stretching into the distance in all its beauty. While we were sitting there, a majestic container ship came sliding into the harbour.

'Hurrah, here come our New Year's noodles!' the owner shouted.

In town in the pouring rain, the evening drinking had begun; men were staggering to and fro.

'Happy Christmas!' a drunk man shouted.

'Christmas finish!' some women laughed.

At United Church Rest House, most guests are conservatively and neatly turned out. They are '*lotu* people', i.e., practising Christians, and orderly in their manner. They would be called 'middle-class' if Solomon Islands had any classes. The men cook, wash, iron and carry babies. The last-mentioned I have seen everywhere in Polynesia and Melanesia.

Among the guests there was an elderly pastor and his wife from Choiseul, both so nice. The wife confirmed Solomon Islands' big problems: the population explosion and the drinking. We touched on the unexplainable, other powers like sorcery, and they confirmed that 'things happen'. They meant it to be part of themselves as islanders and something they must take into consideration, even as Christians. But the wife told me that one time, a foreign doctor had terrible pains after having visited a *taboo* place. Everybody assumed that it was the punishment of the ancestral spirits, but it was actually kidney stones. ('Taboo' is a word in common for Oceanic languages and means 'forbidden', 'sacred', 'untouchable'. It is a central concept in Pacific culture.)

New Year's Eve morning we were sitting in the dining room. It was, and is, so beautiful. The walls are covered with finely woven pandanus mats in decorative patterns and with graceful fish bone-shaped ceremonial spears in dark wood. During breakfast the couple's son and his Japanese fiancée came visiting. They were getting married the following week and were so sweet together: young, in love, and hopeful for the future. He was very dark, with powerful features, she very light, with a complexion like low-fat milk, transparently white. Then a young man with an East Asian appearance arrived. Her brother? No, a Korean. He would participate in the wedding and represent her family, since her real family had rejected this cross-cultural alliance. The clerical couple, on the other hand, had accepted the girl with open arms.

'As long as they love each other and she respects his culture,' was their attitude.

There are many Japanese-Solomon marriages, but many also split up. The pastor's wife was concerned but would pray for the young couple. And some years later I met them again, still married and with three little boys.

I could feel how tired I was. Tired body, tired head, tired of social contacts. The security guard Samson tried to converse but only got occasional words out of me. I went to bed at nine every evening, sometimes earlier, and would like to sleep always. I could not stand the talkative Solomon Islanders with their friendliness, despite these being characteristics that I like so much. I had been travelling half of my allotted time. I was not homesick for Sweden, but neither I had yet felt fully at peace. I had had stimulation, excitement, experiences, yes, but not inner peace for a long time. Had there been any place where I really had felt that?

At midnight I woke up because of the noise. What, what? Oh yeah, New Year's Eve! I hurried up to the veranda. In town they were letting off fireworks: sparkling rockets, red suns, artificial stars. Church bells were ringing, people were driving around in cars, shouting and honking. The security guard was sleeping on the veranda but woke up with the noise, too. It would have been nice to wish Happy New Year to somebody. But we were alone in the whole house, and it felt suddenly too intimate to acknowledge each other's presence. But at least I *saw* some celebrations. Happy New Year 2007!

New Year's Day. Public holiday and everything closed. Would these holidays never have an end! I took a long walk. Hungry! A Chinese kai-bar came to my rescue. The next day, a Tuesday, I was going to Gizo.

Gizo

It would be one of *those* days again. Quite happy, I got up at five and walked down to the harbour to take *Solomon Express*. The boat was there as it should have been, only it wasn't going to Gizo but to Auki. Change of route! I showed them my ticket, dated that very day to Gizo, but they just said 'sorry'. The next boat to Gizo would depart on *Friday*! Several other passengers were just as lost as I and did not know what to do.

I tried to sit down at a kai-bar to think, but there were drunkards swarming around, women and men, old and young. Ouch, how annoying they were. No, I had to get out from Honiara immediately. I raced around, a bus here and a bus there, and at last I managed to get a ticket to Gizo from another shipping company, *Pelican*. Departure next day. And a refund from *Solomon Express*.

Now, in a souvenir shop I bought something I had wanted all the time: a Nguzunguzu image. The image symbolises a spirit in Western Province: god of sea, god of travel and god of war. Nguzunguzu can take various shapes: a human being, a dog or a bird. In the olden times, the warriors attached it on the bows of their war canoes as a charm and protector. My image was made of wood with beautiful inlays of mother-of-pearl, a 10 cm high human head with harmonic features and a little smile, and I felt it was benevolent and wished me well. Its human shape appears on the Solomon 1-dollar coins.

Photo 5

Wednesday morning. Let's try again. Yes, I really set off this time, on the *Pelican* and on time, even. A twelve-hour boat voyage was expected. The day's order looked like this: First I was sitting in the air-conditioned rear salon, watching the other passengers and video action, trying to read (an English novel, but it felt totally out of place, so I gave up) and slept. When it became unbearably cold, I went up to the rear deck under a roof of blue acrylic Plexiglas, watching the passengers and the fabulous archipelago with little emerald-green islets; I slept again. There I kept sitting until it became unbearably hot; then I started from the beginning again. Each pass took around two hours, and so went the day. I was musing:

Sitting and dangling my legs outside the rail. I am on my way in a war canoe with Nguzunguzu attached to the bow.

Studying people. Here in the west, they look different than in Malaita in the east. They are dark brown, some almost black, with gracile features. Some Polynesians, some Chinese, but not one single one like me. It is not surprising that the children stare.

Beside me, three neat men were reading a thick compendium about electrification on the islands. Opposite me, an old man was husking a coconut with his *teeth*. He spit the skins over the rail. The wind caught them, and they slapped a Chinese passenger in his face. He flinched and looked upwards, annoyed, as if it came from a bird. Only I and another passenger saw the little drama, and we smiled in mutual understanding. Smiled, yes, most Melanesians smile at the slightest contact with flashing white or red-stained teeth, with a nod or only with raised eyebrows.

We berthed at mini-harbours on the islands; the ship deposited passengers and cargo like a hen lays eggs, mostly sacks with rice but also canisters with oil, cartons, a coiled water-hose and much more. Everything comes from the Chinese-owned stores in Honiara. The two speed boat companies are Chinese-owned, too. Many Melanesians are annoyed at this economic dominance, which was one of the reasons behind the burning of Chinatown in April 2006.

In Gizo I got a bed at Rekona Hostel, where I met the Australian Lloyd and the German Sabina. As I wanted to go to Munda, Lloyd showed me the place in the harbour where boat transport departs a few times a week. In the evening we went to Gizo Hotel, where they had a dance performance with a troupe from a nearby community, originally re-settled from Kiribati in Micronesia. Kiribati is said to have the best dances in the region: a very pleasant style similar to that of Polynesia and with the women dressed in *green* grass skirts, not yellow or pale brown like in Polynesia.

We had a luxurious dinner with fried fish in coconut milk and bush-lime. And quite a lot of beer. It was time to play a tourist a little. It is difficult for a single woman to have a beer or two in Honiara, let alone in Malaita. This would be my New Year's dinner. But there were reper-cussions – at night I thought the ceiling-fan was a helicopter.

The next day I tried in vain to call Agnes Lodge in Munda to book a room. Was there anything wrong with the telephone? I called Our Telekom's Customer Service:

'I'm trying to call a number.'

'Which number?'

'A number in Munda.'

'Yes, but which one?'

'61133.'

'It is changed to 62133.'

She didn't even look it up.

In the evening there was a new dance performance at Gizo Hotel, now with a troupe from Central Province with male war dances. Young boys with painted, almost naked, bodies were dancing to the music from five-meter-long bamboo panpipes. They, that is the panpipes, not the boys, were so big that they lay on the floor, while the musician was sitting on top. This was followed by a Micronesian dance with the women sitting on the floor. This type of 'sitting-dance' I had seen earlier in French Polynesia.

After this, some sturdy women in hibiscus dresses continued. Side by side they were jumping in a fast rhythm with the music. In between they were standing on the spot, shaking their big bodies and laughing till they howled. They pulled up the onlookers and squeezed them so hard that it was impossible for them not the follow the rhythm. One man was unwise enough to follow the very biggest one. She shook him like a glove.

Gizo was a nice little town, with a bustling market in the harbour. But three months later, the town was hit by an earthquake which caused a tsunami. The town was reduced to rubble, and 52 persons died. Horror stories tell about people who, unaccustomed to this kind of catastrophe, were late in going to high places. Gizo is rather hilly, so it would have been easy. When they realized it at last, it was too late; the water caught up with them...

Munda

The next morning, I boarded the boat Araka to Munda. It was an open motorboat with 12-14 seats but without any shade from the sun. We set off, albeit a little delayed. However, after a while the driver began to ponder, checked the passenger list and discovered that he had forgotten one passenger! The boat turned and picked up the hapless individual.

It was a nice voyage; we were seated on boards, and the wind was blowing. I slept a little. But a beer-drinking young guy with Rasta hairdo was getting more and more noisy. His friends apologized, first for the delay and then for the noisy guy.

We were passing Soltai's big fish industry in Noro and stopped in their little harbour. Most passengers disembarked, and after a little more than two hours altogether we arrived at Munda.

Munda is situated on the island of New Georgia and has a bright, airy view over the sea and the lagoon. Agnes Lodge was a true pearl, a nice resort with everything from bungalows to dorms, a shop, an office for Go West Tours, a big, big bar and a restaurant. The guests were both tourists and locals. I immediately had a dip in the sea, and thus swimming around in the water, I made up my mind on the spot to stay in Munda a little longer. Sabina from Gizo had arrived, too, and together we watched the red sunset from a bench at the beach.

The next morning, I woke up early and padded out onto the jetty. The lagoon looks like an archipelago in south-east Sweden, with islets and boat jetties, but with palms.

Munda has a pleasant market, where you can buy banana pudding for breakfast and chew betel nut with the female vendors. The 'centre' consists of three Chinese stores, a restaurant, a police station, a bank, an Our Telekom-office and by that time, indeed, an airstrip and a truly tiny terminal. It was even open, even if the two staff members lay sleeping on the benches. I woke up one of them and managed to book the last seat for Munda to Honiara for the following week. (In 2015, this dirt airstrip and mini-terminal expanded and was upgraded to an international airport!)

The area around Munda presents the treats of Roviana Lagoon, the island of Nusa Roviana (nusa = island) with the sacred stone dog, the waterfall Holopuru Falls and Kundu Island with human skulls. Go West Tours offered to arrange tours, but everything is so expensive when you are alone. The kind manager gave me ideas how I could arrange it myself.

Nusa Roviana with the stone dog

In the 'good old times', the whole of New Georgia was known for head-hunting. Life was insecure, with eternal warfare between neighbouring ethnic groups. The men who were killed in a fight lost their heads. The contents were eaten; the skulls were smoked, cleaned and kept. The head was the location of mana and the most important part of the body. The women of the conquered group were taken as child-breeding slaves, but the children who were born were declared free.

The Roviana were the strongest and most aggressive group in New Georgia. According to oral tradition, their war canoes could be paddled all the way down to Guadalcanal in their raids, a distance of 250-300 km. At Nusa Roviana they built a fortress, of which the ruins still remain. It was the English colonizers who, in their attempt to stop the head-hunting, destroyed the fortress and burned every house in Roviana.

I went for a visit to Nusa Roviana, together with Sam, a Roviana man I had met at Agnes Lodge. He paddled me from Cape Ilangana across Roviana Lagoon to Nusa Roviana. In the middle of the lagoon he offered me sex. Not flirty or aggressively, just to be informative. I declined politely.

At Nusa Roviana, Sam took me to the guide, a man who owned some historical stone axes. He offered to show them for a fee, but I declined. However, I paid kastom fee, the fee for entering the land and guidance to the fortress with the stone dog. The three of us – Sam, the guide and I – walked up a path, along 'gardens', cultivations, with a dizzying view over the lagoon and continued into the bush. It was impenetrable at times; the guide cut a path with a *bush knife*, the obligatory sabre-like jungle knife with a half meter long blade. The first ruins consisted of stone walls which had progressively collapsed and surrendered to the green moss and the mould. On the walls we saw whole skulls, pieces of skull bones, shells of giant clam shells as well as New Georgia's variety of shell money, *bakiha* – massive polished rings of mussel shells, 10-20 cm in diameter. One example of bakiha appears on the Solomon 2-dollar coins.

The whole path was covered with small seashells which cracked under our steps. The Rovianans used to gather the shellfish for food and then put the empty shells on the paths, so that they could be warned of enemies with their cracking. There followed several stages of stone walls and cairns, upwards, upwards, and on the very top was the most sacred: a little altar in the jungle with a giant clam shell, a conch shell, a bakiha, some pieces of skull bone and then the sacred stone dog. The wild dog used to be the totem of the Roviana, and therefore they had carved this little image. The stone dog was a guardian. It used to twist his head in the direction where the enemies were approaching, it was said.

Now only the head remained, a little pathetic head of some 10 cm in size, surrendered to the moss and the mould, too. The legend tells that an early missionary, in his anger over this pagan artefact, had thrown the stone dog down the slope, where it was crushed. Only the head had been found and returned. Afterwards, the perpetrator had been struck down with an unexplainable illness and died. Later, I heard other varieties of this story, and the timing became murkier. One variety tells about children who were playing and happened to break the stone dog. Some years ago, or 10-20 years ago, or in the 19th century. But in all cases, it led to malevolent and sudden death.

The air was totally still; the jungle was steaming. The altar and the little head were imposing and touching. We cleaned up some of the leaves and rubbish, stood quietly for a while and went back.

The guide had seemed irritated all the time and had not said anything at all. I supposed he didn't speak English. But now he turned to me and asked in fluent English,

'Do you live with that man?'

'No!'

Sam had apparently said that I did. Anyway, Sam paddled me back across the lagoon, and we returned to Munda. I was getting annoyed with him, as he told everyone we met that I lived with him.

Holopuru Falls

The Holopuru Falls waterfall should have been situated just close to Munda, and I had really tried to find my way there, along gardens with *hedges* of phalaenopsis orchids, but I had to give up. It was hard to ask, and when I did, I received conflicting information. So now again, I went by bus as far as I could and continued by foot. The road was brand-new and recently asphalted, a broad new road for heavy vehicles. It should take half an hour, but I walked and walked without end. Further on, I heard axe blows meaning there was a human being to ask, and indeed, a woodsman confirmed,

'Oh yes, this is the way to the waterfall!'

But when? The sun was right in zenith and drilled its beams over the poor wanderer. In spite of my umbrella, the heat was almost unbearable. After an hour I sat down on the asphalt, feeling hopeless. Was I going the right way? Would I have to give up again?

If this had been a movie, then a car would have appeared about now with happy people ready to give me lift, or something similar. And really, out of the sun-flecked road, two figures appeared: a man and a woman. I greeted them:

'Good morning! Is this the way to the waterfall?'

'Yes! Do you want to see the waterfall? We can take you there.'

Now I saw that on their backs they had white, shimmering wings, and around their black frizzy hair a radiance, a halo, was clearly visible. They were Angels. Otherwise, they looked like ordinary people: Middle-aged, the man was wearing shorts and a worn t-shirt, the woman had a patterned skirt pulled up over her bosom and bare shoulders. The couple, Joel and Maylyn, were coming from their gardens. The man was also a boat driver for Go West Tours.

We walked just a quarter of an hour and then turned into a little path after a small bridge. I would have *never* found that path myself. It was completely overgrown. The man went first and cut his way with his long bush knife, *swish-swash*. After yet another quarter of an hour we reached the falls in a glade in the jungle. The falls were low; they were leaping slowly down the mountainside and formed little bubbling, rippling pools. Children were playing, jumping and diving. We the adults bathed, too. I was overheated and had never felt such a physical delight as when the cool water was enclosing me. We were splashing and laughing when our clothes filled with giant air bubbles.

On the way back we went together to the point where I had met them. Still up until today, I don't know where they were actually going. Maybe they just wanted to try out the new road, which they said was only two days old. And the woman had never seen the falls. I gave them $30, the approximate charge for a half day's guiding. Now I had only a 'short walk' to Agnes Lodge, they said. It took more than an hour. They go on a 'short walk' like that every day.

Skull houses on Kundu Island

The little island of Kundu is a ritual site of human skulls. To get there I engaged Go West Tours, the simplest way. It is so troublesome to arrange everything oneself. The boat trip took 20 minutes, and the driver was Joel, who had shown me the waterfall. A guide was also with us. On the shore of Kundu, an old man, Mr Eddie, was collecting the kastom fee. He was skinny and withered and looked like a skull himself, with black skin drawn tight over his cheek bones. But he had the twinkle in his eye; we were joking in my homemade Pijin.

I took a nice photo of three generations of Solomon Islanders: the young guide with trendy sport clothes and sunglasses, the middle-aged boat driver with an Agnes Lodge emblem on his t-shirt and the aged skull tender. No, he was not dressed in a loincloth but in shorts and a t-shirt with the text 'Taman War & Reptilia Malaysia'. Islanders here have the most peculiar t-shirts, from all over the world. You may think they have travelled a lot, but the explanation is rather to be found in the innumerable second-hand shops with clothes donated from Australia.

Now I had three guides. All over the island you could see walls and on them and inside cavities were skulls, mussel shells and shell money from 300 years ago, up to the 1920's. The skulls came both from their own chiefs and from enemies. Via the heads one thus came to be in possession of the power inside, mana. On a wall I saw a skull house, a triangle-shaped sarcophagus of stone with carved patterns, holding the most revered skulls of their own chiefs. The most important was that of Chief Higava, the one who resisted the missionaries longest of all.

Later, I visited the photo exhibition at the airstrip. An old yellowed black and white photo from 1907 showed Chief Higava, an imposing and unusually tall man with unmistakable status. He was standing beside his spear-carrying men beside a war canoe. The five-meter-high bow, where they used to attach Nguzunguzu, was decorated with mother-of-pearl-inlays. He himself looked straight into the camera, eyeing the photographer, not smiling but neither hostile. And now I had been standing at his skull, so close that I could have touched it.

Honiara revisited

The last day I had dinner in the little Jevisa Restaurant, which had just as delicious food as Agnes Lodge but cheaper. They had a beautiful garden, sort of out of the way and somewhat hidden. At the time for departure, I walked the ten minutes to the airstrip and checked in. The plane was the attraction of the day, and the whole town was there to watch. So *swish*! we were off over the coconut palms, and after some stop-overs we arrived in Honiara. It was almost dark when I stepped in at United Church Rest House.

There I met the clerical couple from Choiseul again, and over a cup of tea they showed photos from their son's wedding in the octagon Wesley United Church. The honeymoon couple had already taken off to Australia, where they were going to live. I shared my dorm with a very interesting woman, Rhoda Sikilabu. She had left a well-paid job in

Honiara – a luxurious life with a washing machine, somebody told me – and moved back to her home village to live a simple life. She was now elected into the provincial parliament in the Isabel Province and was trying to start a sawmill in her village. She told of how she had been invited to a Women Parliamentarians International Conference in Rwanda in February. One year later, when we met in the street, she talked about different women's projects she had afoot.

Three tourists had arrived at United Church Rest House: two Finns and one Spaniard. It was a positive meeting; it is fun to meet tourists from time to time. But the Spaniard had lost his checked baggage on the flight; he had kept USD 2,000 in it. In the *checked* baggage!!??

Rhoda went back to Isabel after having sent a petrol drum onto the ship. I gave her my green lavalava, and she gave me earrings of green seashell. I helped her to the ship with all her belongings. At night, I had a restless sleep, due to lots of insect bites.

Last day in Honiara. I was walking very slowly, enjoying every little corner and nook in town, feeling the spicy scent of betel nut. I was pondering a lot. On one hand, it was time to go on and leave Melanesia; on the other hand, I wondered how I would manage without Honiara for the rest of my life. My mood was melancholy. The next day I would fly to Micronesia: Marshall Islands, then Nauru, then Kiribati, then Fiji.

To and Fro in the Pacific

Marshall Islands, Micronesia

Micronesia, but actually only Marshall Islands, but actually only the main atoll Majuro, but actually only the piece of land Rita where the capital Delap-Uliga-Djarrit (DUD) is situated, became a different experience. Not completely pleasant.

Gone were the green mountainous volcanic islands; here you had flat atolls with meagre limestone. They reminded me of the atoll islands in French Polynesia, but even more meagre, more barren and more bare. The only road in Majuro is built on the reef, and in some places there is only the deep sea on one side of the road and the lagoon on the other. The highest point in Majuro is seven metres. If there is a tsunami, that's it. It brings a feeling of vulnerability.

Still, the people in the Pacific know how to protect themselves. Once, a cyclone struck Tikopia, an island within Solomon Islands. The world around thought that all life was extinguished, as the rescue helicopters saw only destroyed houses and crops but no people. But when the cyclone had passed by, the people crawled out from their holes. They had dug themselves down.

Majuro looks like a dot on the map. But the whole atoll, including the lagoon, is around 30 by 10 km, i.e., 300 km². And Majuro is only the main atoll in the huge nation of Marshall Islands. One may object that most of the nation consists of water, which cannot be counted. *But water must be included in a country's surface*. Water means transport, raw material resources and working places. Not counting the water would be as if one, on a continent, would not count highways, mines, forests or deserts. The maritime boundaries of a nation are set as Exclusive Economic Zones (EEZs).

Marshall Islands has a total area of land and EEZ of c. 2.1 million km². For Australia, that is almost exactly the combined area of New South Wales, South Australia and Victoria. For Europe: France, Germany, Spain, Sweden and United Kingdom (combined). For the USA: Arizona, California, Montana, New Mexico and Texas (combined). The question of water is a central issue for Pacific Island nations, not the least due to climate change, and these days they tend to call themselves Large Ocean States rather than Small Island States – rightly.

I stayed at The Flame Tree, with a lovely sunset beer veranda, and met Brian from the USA and Peter from Switzerland. They would also go to Kiribati, in the same flight as I.

Here in Marshall Islands there isn't much to do, if you don't have access to a sailing boat. Sailing and diving are the tourist activities here. I had to be content with strolls on the atoll. But in spite of the lack of activities, I learnt maybe more about the Pacific here than anywhere else. The greatest benefit from my time in Marshall Islands ('but actually only the main atoll Majuro', etc.) was what I gleaned from all that I read. At the Tourist Office I saw some old issues of the magazine *Pacific*, which I devoured greedily. And in the little Alele Museum I learnt about the first people in the Pacific. (The dating below is adapted to recent research, but it is still rough and under debate.)

The Pacific began to be populated about 60,000 to 40,000 years ago, when hunter-gatherers from south-east Asia spread over the present Papua New Guinea and Australia. The latter became the ancestors of the Australian Aborigines.

The next large wave began around 5,000 years ago, when Papuan-speaking people from south-east Asia moved eastwards via Papua New Guinea. The newcomers had knowledge about farming and canoe-building.

A third wave, again from south-east Asia, probably from the present Taiwan, were Austronesian-speaking settlers with advanced knowledge of agriculture and seafaring. Some branches moved southwards towards the present Melanesia and could have reached the present Solomon Islands 3,500-3,000 years ago. They mixed gradually with the Papuans to form today's Austronesian-speaking Melanesians. But there are still some pure Papuan-speaking descendants in Solomon Islands, e.g., in the island of Savo.

The Lapita culture appeared during this time with their pottery with advanced geometrical decorations. It is under debate if these people were Polynesians or Melanesians.

Other branches, the would-be Polynesians, continued eastwards and reached what is now Tonga around 1300 BCE. Samoa, called the Cradle of Polynesia, is estimated to be the first island inhabited by pure Polynesians in 1000 BCE. Hereafter, Polynesians continued eastwards. They reached French Polynesia in the first millennium CE. Some continued to Rapa Nui, the present Easter Island. Some moved north-wards towards Hawai'i and finally some southwards towards Aotearoa, the present New Zealand, which they reached in 1100 CE. Some

Polynesians even turned westwards, c. 1200-1600 CE, i.e., back to Melanesia, which their ancestors had left.

In the same building as the museum was the library, well-kept, with a special Pacific room. There I tried to dig out everything that seemed interesting about Polynesia, Melanesia, Micronesia: colonial depictions, research reports and modern travel books... I kept reading, reading about everything I had been sensing and feeling, but not been able to express in words.

Captain James Cook found in Aneityum, Vanuatu 'a low technological level [...] but a high degree of social courtesy and cultural harmony'.

Michael Lieber expressed Melanesian identity in the following way: 'The person [in Melanesia] is not an individual in the Western sense of the term. [...Instead he is] a locus of shared biographies: personal histories of people's relationships with other people and with things'.

The group's consensus is more important than the individual's wishes. Fear of conflict. Melanesia is no place for climbing the career ladder.

Arthur Coates pointed out the importance of 'truthfulness and cooperation' in Vanuatu and Solomon Islands societies. In Fiji they embrace the principle 'Stay in your own position', i.e., 'Know your place or don't be a tall poppy'. Humbleness, modesty, minimizing oneself. I kept reading. Everything started to fall into place.

When I returned to The Flame Tree there was a message waiting:

Ann & Brian
Due to mechanical problems, your flight is delayed until Friday. We apologize for the delay. Thank you.
Air Nauru

'Your flight' was the next day, Tuesday! Three days' delay! In my ears the words by my German friend Eckart, when his sister and I were stranded in Samoa, were echoing:

'I understand that in the Pacific, delays are not measured in hours but in days.'

Peter was furious over the delay. He added,

'Even if the plane takes off, you can never be sure if it will land.' I myself shrugged, I had become used to the Pacific uncertainty and slow pace.

What to do now? The country's only library was closed, as the librarian was ill. Instead I went to the Land Archives on the ground floor and met an interesting person: Amram Enos.

Amram was leading a project called Micronesian Resources Study, about preservation of Micronesian culture. He stated in a report:

In contrast to Euromericans and Europeans, Micronesians define historic preservation not unlike many Native American groups. [...] In Micronesia, historic preservation involves more than historical places; it includes oral history and oral literature, art forms, music, dance, ceremonies, and perhaps most importantly, traditional values and beliefs. [...] Historic places [...] are physical links to traditional beliefs, traditional forms of social and political integration and traditional values.

Next day was the magic Friday, and I would *perhaps* fly to Kiribati... And just as I feared, there would not be any Kiribati for me. At the airport I, as a Swedish citizen, was asked for a visa to Kiribati: 'new rules from New Year'. Which I didn't have. What do I do now? I could either go back to Majuro, apply for a visa and wait. Hmm. Or fly back to Honiara. Yes! Yess!!

Airport officials had to recheck me and change the baggage tags. The prospect of returning to Honiara made me dizzy with joy. I was ecstatic and babbled to some Solomon women about how happy I was. I felt warm in my heart when I saw some passengers with Melanesian faces.

Full of optimism, I boarded the plane. But when we made a stopover in Nauru, we found a large group of Solomon students stranded by the cancellation of Tuesday's flight. The airport had to charter a plane to fly them over to Fiji. Guess which plane? Yes, *ours*.

They offered a free sightseeing tour around Nauru, so at least I saw something of this country. Then there was wait, wait, and after *ten* hours we finally set off for Honiara. Now surely there could be no more obstacles. But after landing in Honiara, there were no buses running, and I had no money for a taxi, and the currency office was closed, and the ATM machine did not work. Luckily, I got a lift with a co-passenger to Chinatown, where I checked in at my old Bulaia Lodge. It was nice to see was nice to see the staff again: Shirley, Peter, Kelly, Joe and all the others – they laughed at me. Ann back again.

Back in Honiara

I was back in Honiara, I was back in Honiara. In spite of social and other problems, it was clear that this was my country; here I must be. In no other country had I felt such a peace.

I was walking slowly along Mendana Avenue and enjoyed what I saw. People in a never-ending stream strolled leisurely up and down the street. Many of them were barefoot; their broad, sturdy feet had never even *seen* shoes. Others wore flip-flops and yet others had jogging shoes or military boots. The boots became sweaty in the humid heat but were fashionable. The men wore shorts and a t-shirt, except government officials who wore long trousers and a shirt. The women wore a skirt to their knees, or shorts, a t-shirt or a blouse, often sleeveless. People were moving slowly; not a single one was in a hurry. The street was red-stained from betel nut gobs, and the air was filled with aromas of rotting fruit and sewage. But still. I was here. Music from the latest CD, *Sisiva* by the Isabel Sisters, was floating in the air.

It had been raining almost all day and the streets had been transformed into puddles, some quite deep. The people were stepping between the puddles with bare feet. The pavement was rough and only partly cemented. In the roundabout at Honiara Hot Bread Kitchen and Anglican Church was the 'hole of annoyance'. It was a big pothole filled with water after every rain. In order to avoid it, you must either balance on the kerb or step into the carriageway, risking your life, or climb on a fence. It took two days for the pothole to dry up, but before that, it would rain again. Later, they filled the 'hole of annoyance' and cemented the whole pavement. But to *get* to the pavement, you must pass a pothole...etc.

At my favourite blue café Amy's I sat for a long time sipping coconut water through a straw. At the market I bought coconuts, *pawpaw* (papaya), banana, *five-corner* (carambola, star-fruit) and a pudding of banana and the root crop *cassava*, wrapped in banana leaves. Five-corner is my favourite. I went to Bulaia with my treasures. I ate half of the pudding for lunch, and the other half I put in the fridge. A few hours later it was gone. Shirley blamed cats, big cats with two legs, who can open a fridge.

I liked both my homes in Honiara. Bulaia Lodge was a bit shabby, but it was bohemian and relaxed. When I felt tired of all their rubbish, I moved over to the United Church Rest House. It was clean and neat, located in the centre of the city with an incredible view over the harbour. But when their strict Christian views became a little too obvious for me, I moved back to Bulaia Lodge again, and so I kept going.

And now I was staying at Bulaia Lodge again. Most of the new guests were male primary school teachers undergoing further training. They would have an exam the coming Monday. In the evening I talked with a man I had met in Auki. I told him about the Swiss doctors, those who wanted to gain respect through shouting and threatening, and he confirmed my concerns.

'Yes, you see,' he said, 'you don't need to be aggressive to gain respect.' True.

The evening was calm; everybody was busy preparing for the exam. I fell asleep early but woke up in the middle of the night and padded out. The TV was on full but nobody cared; everybody was sitting in a little group on the floor talking with mild Melanesian voices.

During the week I became more familiar with the society and was able to increase my number of contacts. With James from the United Church Rest House I walked through the charming Fijian Quarter neighbourhood, named after the Fijian settlement in the 19th century. It is nestled between hills and embedded in soft greenery with banana plants, palms, low houses and meandering paths. At Bulaia Lodge we met James' friends, Piko and Anta, an older couple and their grandchild, the eight-year-old Emma. Anta was quiet-spoken, bright and nice but didn't speak English, and I had not learnt Pijin yet. They offered bread, *tayio* (tinned tuna) and beer and we had a pleasant evening. Later on, we had a tour by taxi, including visiting the Parliament, where we admired the illuminated view of Honiara.

Piko, Anta and James were living examples of the population in Solomon Islands. Piko was from Western Province, very dark-skinned, Anta from Guadalcanal and medium dark, James from Temotu was a light-skinned Polynesian. And I was, in spite of my suntan, remarkably pale beside the others.

At Bulaia Lodge I also met Ania, a young woman with sad eyes. She was 18 years old, married, with a little daughter of four months. Her belly was a bit round...yes, she was four months pregnant, expecting twins.

Mi go hard life, she said and sent off a red betel nut gob.

University of South Pacific (USP) Campus Solomon Islands, is situated in Chinatown, just beside the sports stadium Lawson Tama, and surrounded in greenery. There are some low buildings with an auditorium, a library, notice boards with exam results and an unmistakable student atmosphere. Around me, the students were busy with group projects or preparations for exams. In the University Library, I eagerly went through their Pacific shelves. I continued to the Public Library and National Library at the Mataniko Bridge in my hunger for books. But at National Library they were changing their catalogue system, and it was terribly messy and dusty, so I left.

I had to confirm my ticket to Fiji and went to Guadalcanal Travel Service (GTS). But there was only one flight a week. I had either to fly the next day or the next week. The next day! Tomorrow! Help! I felt absolutely unprepared for leaving Solomon Islands... But sooner or later I must go... so it might as well be tomorrow. Now I had a lot to do.

Earlier, at the United Church Rest House, I had met Rhoda, the woman from Isabel. Now she had been interviewed by the journalist Julian Maka'a for the newspaper *Island Sun*. I decided to go and see the journalist at Solomon Island's news agency *One News*. When I told him about my travels and my thoughts about Melanesia, he was so interested that he wanted to interview me for TV. He did so, and in the evening, I appeared on the TV news! I talked about my deep respect for Solomon Islands and about everything I had been thinking and experiencing. You cannot say so much in five minutes, so I promised Julian I would develop my thoughts for a larger newspaper article.

Julian is a dynamic person who, in addition to being a journalist and a writer, for some time was responsible for the National Disaster Management Office, an organisation started after a severe earthquake.

At the United Church Rest House, I shared my room with an anthropologist from the USA. Together we went for a beer at Quality Inn (nowadays named Rock Haven Café), where she told me about her frustrations with the Ministry of Commerce, Industries, Labour and Immigration, regarding her permits.

The next morning was my last day. Everything was set. I strolled along the harbour for the last time, bought earrings at the market and the *Sisiva* CD. All my money was finished; there was just enough for the bus to the airport and the airport tax. The United Church Rest House was so empty; everybody was gone. I felt sad. Lonely I arrived, lonely I left.

After I had checked in, my stomach cramp disappeared; I was on my way again. In the departure hall, I saw Vivianne, a woman I met while waiting in Nauru. She owns a gift shop at the airport, and I could not resist the temptation to buy a lavalava, although I already had so many. It was a purple one with the text: SOLOMON ISLAND THE UNTOUCHED PARADISE.

Bula Fiji

Fiji. Geographically and ethnically Fiji is Melanesian; culturally rather a mix of Polynesian 'pomp' and Melanesian simplicity. The strong Indian element, almost half the population, and the many tourists definitely give their own character to the country. I arrived in the evening in Nadi. Nadi is not the capital, but it houses the main international airport.

It was my third visit to Nadi, and I moved into my old Nadi Hotel in the town centre. Unfortunately, they had removed the *masi* decorations in the dining-room, the beautiful Fijian bark work, also called *tapa*, which is the most elaborate and sophisticated in the entire Pacific.

That night I sat straight up in the bed. Fiji has so much to give, but I felt no joy; everything seemed so meaningless. What had I done by leaving Solomon Islands? Why did I not stay one more week? There remained so many questions in Honiara. I padded out and stood on the stairs in the Fijian night.

Next day, as I was strolling in town, somehow and somewhere I made a decision to return to Honiara. I wasn't finished with that country. At a travel agency I booked a return ticket to Honiara – expensive, ouch. But this was something stronger than me. I felt relieved; now I could really relax and enjoy Fiji.

I chose the tour 'The Jewel of Fiji', with a visit to Koromakawa (= old village), a kind of open-air museum. They were showing pandanus weaving, tapa dyeing, kava drinking of course and much more. The lunch was extravagant: delicious parcels of banana leaves with fish, chicken and spinach pudding in coconut milk. A little group of musicians was sitting on the floor singing mildly melancholic songs accompanied by a guitar. Everyone who has been to Fiji has heard their farewell song, 'Isa Lei'. Finally, dances. This was followed by a boat trip up the Navua River with deep, deep rainforest on both sides, and a swim in the wonderful Magic Waterfalls. The tour ended on a bamboo raft, where we floated slowly downstream to the sound of the murmuring water. It was a wonderful, peaceful experience, and I wished it would never have to end. But it did.

This successful tour operation had won several distinctions, and their name 'The Jewel of Fiji' was very appropriate. It was a true little jewel, composed in harmony with a nice mix of everything and with a personal style.

An important meeting

When leaving Fiji at Nadi Airport I saw the sunrise. A Japanese transit passenger looked out, admired the mountains and asked me which country this was. 'Fiji,' I replied kindly but muttered to myself 'of course'. I was now getting used to flitting to and fro in the Pacific. Just before the stopover in Vanuatu the plane flew very low over Mele Maat, and I saw my little cottage!

Meandering rivers in Guadalcanal. For the third time I arrived at Henderson Airport, the fourth if you count domestic. This was my country. How familiar everything in the arrival hall now seemed! 'Under the trees by the main road', a Scotsman chewing betel nut offered me lift to Honiara. He lived here and said I was crazy to want to move here.

'But you live here!?'

'Yes, I am crazy!'

They were happy to see me at United Church Rest House, not believing that I was back. It was as if I had never been away. They had seen me on TV! Later I was sitting at NPF Plaza. Right there I met a nice old man who humbly asked me for two dollars for juice, because he was so thirsty. And I who had just written in my newspaper article that there were no beggars in Honiara. But this episode doesn't count.

After a few days I longed for Bulaia Lodge and moved over there. They were happy to see me too, and had also seen me on TV, where I said more or less the same thing as in the article.

Strolling slowly along Mendana Avenue, swimming in the human sea. Your fellow beings flashing a 100-watt white-toothed or red-stained smile. Most faces so beautiful: dark, powerful. Skin of every brown hue. The afro-style hair of the Melanesians, bushy or artistically plaited, the soft curls of the Polynesians, the straight hair of the Chinese. Dignified posture, graceful image. Children in neat school uniforms, nuns from different denominations.

Oh yes, there were also annoying sides. But the great, overwhelming question for me was now:

'How on earth will I manage without Honiara for the rest of my life??'

One day I took a minibus with friends to White River, a settlement of islanders from Temotu and Rennell & Bellona, the two Polynesian provinces. They live a very simple life near the sea. A proud mother placed her new-born daughter in my arms. Delighted, I admired the little downy head and the tiny, tiny hands.

One evening I went to Honiara Hotel, opposite Bulaia Lodge. Although it was so close, it was the first time I had been there. It was much fancier than I had expected, and they had dance performances!! It was a troupe from Kiribati. So I had a glimpse of that country after all. They were remarkably colourful and artistic, and stupidly I had forgotten my camera.

The last weekend, whom should I meet but Ronnie, my guide from Malaita. Together with Semi, a Tongan IT-expert, we went to the Yacht Club on Saturday evening. By that time, only members and 'temporary overseas visitors', i.e., foreigners, were welcome, so the black-haired and dark-skinned gentlemen were stopped. Semi was doubtless a foreigner, but Ronnie had to pay $50 to enter – ouch. There were some beers, a rugby match on a bigscreen and a talk about intercultural relations.

Sleepy Sunday! Too much beer last night. In the afternoon, Ronnie invited me with some friends for a picnic. Among them was his cousin, a man I had not met before. Robert. First, we went in the opposite direction to buy beer. It is normally not possible to buy beer on a Sunday, but there is a 'private' (read: illegal) bottle shop... We wanted to rent a taxi for a few hours, preferably a 'taxi with music', but that's not easy on a Sunday either. The tape recorder of the first taxi was broken, and there was a lot of fuss to get another taxi, and when we finally found one, it had only gospel music. The desperate driver tried to call taxi central to find another one 'but-not-gospel'. Taxi central eventually lost patience and shouted 'if they say what music they want, we'll get them a taxi.' I could not follow all the conversation in Pijin but just went along with everything, and at last we set off. At White River we bought grilled fish and cassava and continued westwards to Bonegi Beach, where we had a little party, with fish, beer, music and chat, chat. Robert and I were discussing intercultural relations.

Just outside the shoreline, a half-sunken warship wreck from World War II is visible. The waters north-west off Honiara are known as 'Iron Bottom Sound', because of the many sunken wrecks. Around 50-60 wrecks remain from four countries: Japan, Australia, New Zealand and the USA. A lot of fish have moved into the wrecks, and Bonegi Beach is a popular spot for snorkelling.

At night, Robert and I continued to develop our intercultural relations in practice.

There was an attraction between us, but how do you handle the fact that you will soon find yourself on the other side of the globe with an uncertain return? You had better accept it as a holiday romance. Distance and time will show, etc.

I spent the days at different libraries, researching and writing my newspaper article. I delivered it to Julian Maka'a at *One News*, and it was published in the *Island Sun* (see below). At *One News* I met a volunteer, a Turkish woman who was Muslim and a feminist. She was very critical of Solomon Islands society and their attitude towards women, especially in Malaita, and could not wait to get back to Turkey. But actually, she had never been to Malaita.

In the evening, some of us waved off Ronnie, who was going back to Auki. The quay was a seething mass of activity. The ship was about to be loaded. Loading was done by hand: cases with biscuits, juice, rice sacks, petrol drums, cooking oil, beer. Men formed a chain of five and threw.

Photo 6

Tuesday again – my bonus week in Solomon Islands was over. The last errands in town were done, and I was going back to Fiji. This time I was accompanied to the airport. By Robert. Now it was definitely my last departure from Honiara. I felt sad, but not as miserable as the week before. Many questions now had an answer. Calm.

A Declaration of Love

Abbreviated version of the article published in the newspaper *Island Sun* (February 2007):

The Solomons and the Foreigner – or a Declaration of Love

It is said that the only foreign thing in a foreign country is the foreigner herself. After half a year in the Pacific, to me – a foreigner from Sweden – this is clear: The more I learn about this part of the world, the more I realize how much more there remains to be learnt – through talking to people, studying their literature and being open to new influences.

To use a metaphor: Knowledge is like a globe. The bigger the globe, the bigger the surface bordering on the unlimited space of the unknown. On the other hand, in no other country did I feel so much in harmony with my own values.

The industrialized world may be highly developed on a technological level, but poorly developed when it comes to interpersonal relations and communication, in comparison with so-called non-Western civilizations. In this sense, Solomon Islands, or the Pacific in general, are outstanding.

Never and nowhere else in the world was I struck by such social and cultural grace. Already during his visits, Captain James Cook observed in Vanuatu 'a low technological level [...] but a high degree of social courtesy and cultural harmony.'

People smile at you in the street and greet you, a foreigner, with a 'Good morning', or even sweeter, a 'Good night' in the evening. You feel gloomy, you look up and see a big white-toothed smile – and raised eyebrows – flashing into your face, and your day is saved.

Most relations between people in Solomon Islands seem to circle around one theme – respect. Show respect and you will gain respect. In many cultures, respect is believed to be achieved through aggression. A customer, a client or a team leader may try to gain respect by shouting and threatening. If they try to act in the same way in Solomon Islands, the effect will be the opposite, which many Western expatriates have bitterly experienced. Although the 'Solos' are highly tolerant when the foreigner unintentionally breaks the cultural protocol, they are sharp observers and can easily sense whether a visitor is looking down upon them, or whether she or he is truly trying to learn and understand and to show respect.

To show respect in Solomon Islands is, for example, to be aware of the personal and interactional 'bubble' that everyone keeps around her- or himself. It is considered rude to pass directly in front of a person or – even worse – between two or more persons while in communication. If you must, apologize or bend your head as an excuse that you are forced to break the bubble. All for the purpose of showing respect for the communicative situation.

Another side of respect is the desire to please. Saying 'no' is considered rude, and the Solomons will try everything to avoid this. This could lead to a clash with the so-called Western need for direct information, be it positive or negative.

Social relations seem more important than economic interests. Therefore, the foreigner can stroll peacefully along the street without vendors chasing her and pulling her – even physically – to buy their goods.

The foreigner can exchange a smile and a chat with a Solomon Islander without having to feel like prey, which would be a humiliating situation for both parties. Solomon Islands is a 'poor' country, but still, this humiliating and undignified scenario doesn't appear. And in contrast to New York, London or Paris, there are rarely any homeless or beggars in the streets.

Social problems do exist here, but mostly they are not specific for Solomon Islands, and can be dealt with by others. This article is about what is unique about Solomon Islands.

I find Solomon Islands addictive. This is my perception of the Solomons – if I am wrong you have to convince me.

Ann Lindvall, travel writer

Fiji again

So let's make a new try in Fiji. In Nadi I met three Canadians, and together we went to the little island of Caqalai, outside the main island of Viti Levu. There I met Swedes and could use my own language. I stayed in a traditional palm leaf hut, *bure*.

There wasn't much to do other than swimming, snorkelling or strolling around the small island, which took 20 minutes. Chatting, of course, and eating. This little Fijian-owned accommodation was cosy, but I was restless and wanted to go further. Together with some Fijians and one Slovakian I returned to the main island and waited for the bus to Suva.

So this was the dangerous capital? Judging by the news reports, you might expect some kind of military siege or national emergency, but it was just an ordinary capital. Suva is the largest city in the Pacific, with skyscrapers, bank palaces, huge advertisement boards; people stress and push, even among the Fijians.

The following days I spent at USP Campus Fiji, which is also larger than any other USP Campus in the Pacific. The university was beginning a new semester and was full of activities, information, registration and student counselling. I enjoyed the special student atmosphere with anticipation in the air. For fun, I took a catalogue and asked around about possibilities for employment. Oh yes, was their positive reply, and for further information I got some email addresses. Well, maybe in the future? The well-arranged university library was free to visit, but access to the Pacific Room, the only one that really interested me, required a permission slip for 45 FJD ($\approx$ SBD 140) – ouch. Admittedly, it was valid for a whole month, but that didn't help me for my only week.

The Suva museum, a large wooden building, is situated in a beautiful park. It had, and probably still has, an anthropology department containing models of canoes with pandanus sails, weapons, jewellery, carved *tabua* (whale tooth), and the utmost of all handicraft: elaborately worked bowls for kava preparation and serving. Another department had information about the pre-Christian religion of ancestral spirits and the shark-god Dakuwaqa, about kastom and practices. The Fijian wantok-system, *kerekere*, is limited to one's own family (which can be quite big). There is a special relation between an uncle (mother's brother) and a nephew (sister's son), where the latter has the right to demand anything from the former.

The second floor housed art galleries and an exhibition about the history of the Fijian Indians.

The last part of my stay in Fiji was on the south coast, at Beachouse Resort, and that was less enjoyable. Beachouse was indeed knockout beautiful with bamboo buildings, greenery and a turquoise pool, but all the guests were foreign tourists, most of whom were very young. How, in what way, were they in Fiji? They had zero interest in the country. They might as well be anywhere with sun, swimming and cheap drinks. The resort provided some Fijian elements though: kava drinking, jewellery making using coconut shells, hair plaiting and massage.

Fiji is wonderful in many ways, but I don't like everything. In addition to the mad rush after tourists and their money, there are also other unequal relations. The Indian population with caste views is colliding head-on with Fijian equality. The forms of address with 'ma'am' or 'madam', especially at tourist places and at the university, bother me. A little fawning and *un-Melanesian*.

My last tourist attraction in Fiji was Pacific Harbour with Art Village. Art Village is some kind of open-air museum, which displays, to use *Lonely Planet*'s words, 'some freeze-dried Fijian culture'.

End of Melanesia!

Reunion with Tonga

After Fiji I felt deflated. Now I had definitely left Melanesia. I was going away, away; the journey would soon end. I did not want this!!! In the back of my mind, though, I felt I was being unfair towards the two remaining countries, Tonga and Samoa, and they should get the attention they deserve.

It was my second time in Tonga, so I expected both old reunions and new experiences. The old ones were sightseeing in the capital Nuku'alofa. King Taufa'ahau Tupou IV had died one year before, and in the main streets, around the Royal Palace (which looks like a huge white wooden church) and around public buildings, purple giant bows and mourning draperies were still hanging over the king's portrait. Seeing the sights (the Royal Palace, the Parliament, the Treasury Building and the Vuna Wharf) was accomplished in a few hours. The cultural Tongan National Center looked the same as before.

I went around the main island of Tongatapu by bus. I saw the blowholes again in Mapu'a Vaea as well as the trilithon Ha'amonga 'a Maui. This is a limestone arch called 'Tonga's Stonehenge' and yes, it might have worked as some kind of calendar. I also saw the Royal Terraced Tombs in the old capital Lapaha and the rock formation 'Pigeon's Doorway' in Hufangalupu.

New experiences were Ha'apai archipelago. I had to take a flight to get there. I spent some lazy days on the small island of Uoleva and visited the world's smallest museum in Pangai on the island of Lifuka.

Back in Nuku'alofa, I stayed at Sela's Guest House together with Suzy, a woman from New Zealand. A free shuttle boat took us to the Pangaimotu islet opposite the harbour. They had a bar which was *open* on *Sundays*, and they were even serving *beer*! Indeed, Tonga had changed!

At night I could not sleep and went out onto the balcony. The night was hot. Across the street was a kava house, where men had gathered for fund-raising. They were drinking kava and singing. Reader, have you ever been in Tonga and heard those male choirs? In unison, they were singing soft melancholic songs, which drifted across the street and found their way up to my balcony. How can big and rough men like that produce anything so lovely? Listening to them is like 'being immersed in liquid honey', as an English woman described it.

Intercultural problems in Samoa

The flight to Samoa and Fale'olo airport was short, a little over one hour. We passed the date line, so it was Tuesday for the second time. The shuttle bus to the city charged 30 SAT (≈ SBD 100) – ouch. Eight years ago, it was *seven*! It was with mixed feelings I looked around the road from the airport. So many things in my life had happened here in Samoa. While we were whizzing into the capital Apia, I observed the environment almost with nonchalance.

Samoa had lost its magic, although I used to love Samoa as much as I love Solomon Islands now. Will the magic of Solomon Islands be lost, too? Wise thoughts.

My old hostel 'The Outrigger' now had a complicated name '1898 Princess Tui Inn'. There I met a gay couple, the Englishman Peter and the Samoan To'a. To'a was very social, with the indolent cat-like sensualism that many Polynesians possess and which has enchanted Europeans for centuries. But they had obvious relationship problems.

To'a confided in me. He was ostracised by his strictly religious family, because he refused to marry a suitable girl. He hadn't told them about his relationship with Peter, since he knew it would make everything even worse. He suffered from agony and nightmares.

Peter confided in me, too. We talked about relationships and the contrasts between European and Polynesian views of life. According to Peter, To'a had many 'eccentric peculiarities', while he himself represented 'common sense', as he said. One 'peculiarity': When they were strolling on the beach, To'a would not dare to sit down on the sand. He was afraid that some wicked person would take the print of his seat and use it in sorcery. He was afraid to spit, for the same reason. I had been in the Pacific long enough to find his argument convincing.

But the question is not if an argument is convincing or not, but if you respect the other's point of view. My objection – that the peculiaities of both sides were culture-specific, and that there is nothing like 'common sense' alone – met with no understanding. They had been a couple for two years, but their relationship seemed to be cracking.

Their differences were highlighted when we went together to a dance show at the legendary Aggie Grey's Hotel. The staff have become increasingly snooty over time, especially if you don't order umbrella drinks but only the local beer called Vailima or soda water. We felt cheated because we were short-changed for our drinks. Three reactions arose: Peter was furious and bawled out the waiter, who in turn threw the change on the table. To'a almost crept under the table in shame. He would not have said anything at all to the waiter. And I guess I reacted in between; I would have pointed out the short-change, but politely. Each of us three probably thought that we reacted with 'common sense', according to our backgrounds. Intercultural relations are not easy.

Lalomanu Beach is situated on the south-east corner of the main island of Upolu and may truthfully be called Samoa's most beautiful beach. The year 1999 was my first visit to Lalomanu Beach. At this new visit, the place was hard to recognize. Once, the four little family stays had only a few huts on the beach; now they spilled over the whole beach. So expensive and so over-commercialised. Lalomanu Beach had become the place where tourists go to swim and drink beer. Still, in my mind, these small-scale local businesses are to be preferred over luxury foreign-owned hotels – partly for the economy of the country and partly for the mutual dignity of both the locals and the visitors.

I revisited the Togitogiga Falls and Upolu's sister island Savai'i. Savai'i is definitely worth visiting, if you want to experience 'the real Samoa'. Savai'i is friendlier, more genuine.

The last morning in Samoa I was sluggish; I stayed in bed and browsed through my passport. When I saw the stamps, I wept quietly. The journey was over, over. There was nothing more to say. In the evening the shuttle bus departed for the airport. I could only wish *Tofā soifua*, farewell.

It was a long flight across the Pacific Ocean to Los Angeles and then across the Atlantic Ocean to Copenhagen. Everything was so strange; all Samoans were gone, not to mention Melanesians. I leaned back in the seat in the nationless airspace thinking, thinking. Evening, dusk is falling. The children are splashing and larking in the lagoon. The sea, place of work, place of transport, place of play. The corals live their eternal life. Nguzunguzu is watching over everything and everyone, good and bad. The sea god, the travel god. Polynesia, Melanesia, Micronesia, kumara, shell money, chiefs, motu; it all floats together, whirls up in a wave which breaks on the reef...

Then I landed in Copenhagen, took a train across the bridge to Sweden, and the calendar showed 3rd April 2007. From that moment I would devote all my energy to the thought of return.

PART II: AT HOME!

PART II: AT HOME!

Everyday Life in Honiara

Tristesse

The time I spent in Sweden was like a long tristesse. I felt as if I had been given an anaesthetic. I dragged myself ahead in the street: 'Who am I, what am I doing here, why am I not in Solomons?' Friends and neighbours asked: 'Don't you enjoy *a little* to be back home in Sweden?' In order not to hurt them I withheld my big 'NO! It's awful!!' I had been torn up with the roots from Solomons (it felt like), put in an airplane and let out in Copenhagen with the words: 'You get off here. Go ahead and live!'

Two weeks after my arrival I booked a new ticket back to Solomon Islands. Eight months ahead, how would I be able to wait? The spring was as beautiful as ever. The sloe blooms first, then the apple trees, then cherries, then chestnut, then lilac, but I didn't see them: 'They have nothing to do with me. I Don't Want To Be Here!'

In front of me I saw an endless row of days before I could set foot in Solomons again. I could not speak about anything else than Solomon Islands. How boring I was! How could my friends stand me?

I spent the waiting time by selling a lot of unnecessary belongings and arranged to rent out my flat. For one year... Eight long months passed: a spring, a summer and an autumn. At last it was time for departure...

Honiara in summary

In 29th November 2007 I am back in Honiara, and it is time for a flashback and a little elaboration. Here you will find Parliament, ministries, police, judiciary, telephone companies, internet cafés, post, banks, industries, universities, supermarkets, hotels, nightclubs, disco. (Much of this you will, of course, find in the province capitals, too.) The exact number of inhabitants is difficult to judge, as many people are not registered here. They are squatters, who built their houses on available land but without tenancy or ownership of that land. Others come and go. They stay with relatives for months, or years, take tem-porary jobs to get some cash and then return back home to the village.

The city centre, Point Cruz, consists in principle of a single street, Mendana Avenue. It extends alongside the sea and could have had a beautiful view on the north side over the harbour with all the ships, if it were not for Honiara Bulk Terminal with South Pacific Oil's ugly, ugly cisterns. The same side houses also a filling station, the Tourist Information Bureau and one of the few fancy luxury hotels: Mendana Hotel. The south side of the street is fringed with innumerable Chinese-owned stores and some kai-bars. Down in the harbour: workshops, wholesalers and enterprises, among others the little charming coconut factory Kokonut Pacific. The bay between the city and the harbour houses the Honiara Yacht Club, which has the best sea view and the cheapest beer.

In the eastern part of the city centre you can see Honiara Central Market, just next to the South Seas Evangelical Church and the octagonal Wesley United Church. Further east you can find Honiara City Council and the Cathedral of the Holy Cross. Then follows a bridge, and then you are in Chinatown.

In the western part of the centre you will find the NPF Plaza, a nice shopping centre. Then comes the Central Police Station and the Post Office, but now we are already outside the centre. Opposite the Police Station is the Art Gallery. In 2007 there was a park with a music stage and some pavilions. It was a place for meetings, concerts and ceremonies with handicraft and food stalls.

The huge white complex at Town Ground is a strange building. Originally meant as a rugby stadium, those plans changed, and it was rebuilt into shops and apartments. The white tower houses two *round* apartments! And then there are some new airy luxury hotels with a beautiful sea view: Heritage Hotel and Coral Sea Resort.

The two other fancy hotels are King Solomon Hotel in Hibiscus Avenue, parallel with Mendana Avenue, and Honiara Hotel in China-town. They have dance performances once a week: charming Polynesian *tamure* dances from Rennell & Bellona or panpipes from Malaita.

Between Mendana Avenue and Hibiscus Avenue are some con-necting roads, with or without asphalt. Along Mendana Avenue the minibuses are running in a never-ending race, as well as taxis, trucks, pickups, bicycles, scooters and motorbikes. Private vehicles are apparently everybody's property, to judge from the traffic jams. The pavements are filled with people in a never-ending, slow stream.

Far away east, on the way to Henderson Airport, you can see the sports field Lawson Tama. Farther on comes the suburb of Kukum. And even farther away lies the suburb of Ranadi, mainly an industrial area but also a site of Solomon Islands National University (SINU).

From Honiara city, innumerable roads lead up in the mountains to the suburbs or settlements Panatina Ridge, Naha, Kola Ridge, Borderline, Vara Creek, Koa Hill and many others. Some of them have regular bus routes. Almost all Melanesians live outside the town in unpretentious houses, which they either own or rent. The inner city – say Mendana Avenue and Hibiscus Avenue from Honiara City Council to the Town Ground and their connecting streets – is almost exclusively inhabited by Chinese. They live in flats, usually above the store they own.

This is a difference between Europe and Asia on one side and the Pacific on the other: Europe and Asia have a long tradition of towns and cities, which are places to work and live. In the Pacific, the towns or cities were until quite recently trading stations and exclusively meant for trading, working and shopping. They are empty after business hours.

Honiara city is thus predominantly a place where you work, more or less occasionally. Even though somebody lives year after year in Honiara without visiting her or his village, they see it as a temporary state. Honiara is not *their* town; it is *nobody's* town and need not be loved or taken care of. It may explain the heaps of dirt and rubbish everywhere. 'Home', on the other hand, is always the place of birth, the village where they own the land. The bond to the land is something fundamentally Melanesian. Every individual has a birth right to a part of the village's land, either on the mother's side or the father's.

The city is thus a hotchpotch of temporary inhabitants from all parts of the country. This has changed the communication patterns of the population. The closest kin may not be relatives anymore but friends of school, friends of work, friends of sport. Friendship has been an added as a complement to family bonds, and the daily means of communication is not the local language but Pijin. The mixed marriages are increasing, and for the children born to them, Pijin will be their first language. The city, although small, anonymises its population, de-emphasises ethnic descent and emphasises a Solomon identity. For its good and its bad.

Honiara's general character of a melting pot does not prevent enclaves, with geographically and ethnically homogenous groups. Thus, White River is dominated by Polynesians from Rennell & Bellona, the whole area between Chinatown and Koa Hill by Malaitans, among others Kwaio. My new relatives are Kwaio.

The people in Solomon Islands
Of the 690,000 inhabitants, the largest group, 95%, are Melanesians. Further, there are around 3% Polynesians, predominantly in the islands of Rennell, Bellona, Tikopia and Ontong Java. The remaining 2%

consist of recently immigrated Micronesians, a handful of Chinese, Caucasians and, recently, Bangladeshi. And then there are all the mixes.

Why are so many Melanesians blond, especially children? There have been several attempts to explain this, by the locals themselves. The hair is said to be bleached by the sun, or by the salt water, or by the diet rich in fish, or even by some Scandinavian explorers among the ancestors. This is questionable. Other people in the world live under the sun and in salt water too, and eat fish, but their hair remains black. Now researchers have found the clue: These blonds have a special, unique gene, TYRP1, which exists only in Melanesia and nowhere else in the world. This gene is also assumed to explain the widespread occurrence of albinism in Melanesia.

Photo 7

There are around 70 ethnic groups in Solomon Islands, each with their own language. The national identity is, to say the least, artificial and fragile. Rather than being a country, Solomons is a mini-world of its own, made up of provinces and islands, often discordant, with ethnic groups who less than 100 years ago were practising warfare against each other.

Since Independence in 1978, the regime has been working hard to strengthen the unity and nationhood. But it has not been easy. The ethnic tensions of 1998-2003 are one example. And in 2006, political discontent was directed towards the Chinese minority. They were accused of economic dominance and political interference through bribery. This led to the riots and fires in Chinatown.

Arrival

Two days before my departure from Honiara in February 2007, I had met Robert Arika. During the following months we had sparse contact via (snail) mail and email. At this new arrival I was wondering: Would this become my home country? Would Robert and I be like strangers to each other? Would I even be *met*?

Robert really met me at the airport. He stood on the observation deck and saw me arrive, and the first thing he said was,

'You have become so fat that I didn't recognize you!'

Meant as a compliment, but still... He himself was very good-looking, slim. Meant as a compliment.

Behind a pillar, he placed a quick kiss on my cheek. Traditional Melanesians don't display emotions between the sexes, but at an international airport it is accepted. We smiled shyly; it felt both tense and exciting. We took a taxi to his house, whizzing by Bulaia Lodge, the guest house where we spent the two last days (and nights) before my departure.

We drove through New Chinatown, past Honiara High School and the Seventh-day Adventist Church and stopped in Vara Creek. From there we walked down a grass slope, and there, on the hillside on the other side of the Mataniko River, there was a group of houses, embedded in greenery. He pointed out his. It was the first time I saw it, and I studied it carefully. Would this be my new home, or...? Perhaps a little more rural than I had imagined. But everything was pure happiness anyway.

To get there, you have to pull yourself across the river on a 'floater', a raft, with a rope tied to both sides of the river. It felt a little shaky in the beginning, especially with my heavy baggage. But Robert took it expertly 'on board', or whatever you say about a raft of 1 x 2 meters, pulled us over and carried the suitcases up the hillside to the house. And here I am.

Photo 8

The house

This, our house in Koa Hill, was situated on a hillside and built in traditional style, a 'leaf house'. The skeleton was partly built of rough planks, partly of big sticks joined into a beautiful and strong network. The floor was laid with planks and on them a vinyl carpet. The walls and roof in a leaf-house are sewn up of sago palm leaves, which – laid in a correct way – makes the house absolutely rainproof. The leaves give a golden yellow light which creates a harmonic element in the surrounding greenery. After a few years, the leaf work becomes damaged by weather and wind and needs to be exchanged. But this leaf work was still brand new.

The house had a high ceiling, which gave a feeling of airiness and coolness. It rested on pillars, which is common here. This is practical when the ground underneath the house is uneven, and in our case, there was also a little stream under the house. You can use the space under the house as a nice outdoor room with shade (as our neighbour does) or hang laundry there (as Robert's brother does) or put all kinds of rubbish there, for example planks, worn out tyres, a bicycle, a chicken net, empty petrol drums and much more (as we do), according to taste.

The house was small, around 18 m^2, with two rooms in a row. The inner room was used as a bedroom. The only furniture was a mattress on the floor, a mosquito net and a TV set, if this is now counted as furniture. Oh actually, Robert built a bookshelf of planks for me. We folded the mattress in daytime. Otherwise, the contact with the vinyl carpet would lead to mould. Bed linen and other textiles were stored in nice 'hanging shelves', made of fabric with hibiscus motifs, purchased at the market. I have not seen such hangings in any other country. Our clothes were kept in suitcases, as we practice 'compact living'. I mean, it would be unnecessarily space-demanding to have *both* drawers *and* empty suitcases.

The outer room was much smaller and was used for different purposes. For example, when we had guests, we put a mattress and a low table there. Here also were the important electric gadgets we cannot live without, such as car batteries and an inverter. They convert the sunshine from the solar panels on the roof to electricity. Not much, but enough for light and the charging of mobiles and laptops.

When I arrived at the house for the first time, everything was so neat and well-arranged, and I could see that Robert had cared enough to please me. He managed, with one exception: the lace curtains in the bedroom. A friend of his had given him the advice to hang up lace curtains to cover the leaf walling and to separate the mattress from the rest of the room. To my eyes it looked quite showy, but out of consideration I didn't say anything. And Robert didn't say anything either. Almost a year later we both found out that neither of us really liked the lace curtains, and down they went.

Now we decorated one wall with a beautiful lavalava. The other walls were a wonder of beauty the way they were. Here, islanders are ashamed of simple natural things (as everybody has it), so imported artificial things are fancier. In Sweden, it is (nowadays) the other way around. With the expensive labour force in Sweden, it is manually handcrafted things that are fancy. My relatives find it a little perverse that I admire natural material. But they are flattered anyway.

Interior decorating is one of my interests, but here it was not much to decorate. The only object (except the walling) was maybe the mattress. I covered it with two joined sarongs from Indonesia in yellow, crimson and green, with three pillows in a Chinese flower design in the same colour scheme. Otherwise, I tried to give the decor a Pacific style. In one window hung a polished seashell from Fiji and in the other a traditional pendant from East Kwaio. One wall was covered with a tapa from Tonga and the floor on the veranda with a sitting mat of woven pandanus leaves from Samoa. I had collected those items from my previous travelling.

This was a typical Solomon house. It looked like this when I arrived, and I hardly changed anything. In the veranda we still have a homemade table, with three green garden chairs. The veranda sometimes serves as a kitchen, with a gas burner. We are the only ones who sometimes cook with gas. Otherwise we have an outdoor cooking house, where we use firewood. Everyone else cooks with firewood.

Photos 9-10

Solomon houses are built with one public and one private area, where guests normally won't go, not even relatives. Even small children learn early that the private area is taboo. On the other hand, there is no invitation needed for the public area; anyone can come and have a seat. Our veranda is the public area. (They used to have that system in Sweden, too, in the olden times. One special beam in the ceiling marked the borderline between the public and the private.)

From the veranda there is a magnificent view over the Mataniko River, running behind banana plants, pawpaw trees and coconut palms with the mountains in the background. And over the ugly toilet shack, the 'small house' as we say here. This part of the river is badly polluted by rubbish heaps and from latrines which go straight out into the water. Plastic bags and bobbing plastic bottles. The metal tins will at least sink.

The household utensils consist of two pots, some deep plates, mugs, cutlery (i.e., spoons and forks, while knives are not used for eating). There are no cupboards or drawers, so everything is put in a drainer rack of red plastic. For grating of coconuts there is a 'scraper', a short board on which you sit while grating. Obligatory is also the bush knife. It is used for everything, from cutting a clearance in the jungle to peeling the root crops and opening tins. (I even saw an old man cutting his toenails with a bush knife.) Some families have a 'small knife', which is everything but a bush knife; it may be a quite big slicer. For dishwashing and laundry there is a bucket or two. This is, I think, standard equipment in a Solomon household.

Since we have no fridge, we cannot store any fresh food, e.g., vegetables or fish; everything must be consumed the same day, or the next. Less sensitive food like coconuts, fruit and root crops, are put in a corner of the veranda or hang in plastic bags under the ceiling to keep it from the rats at night. Inside the house we keep staple food like rice, biscuits, tayio, sugar and salt.

There are trendier shops in Honiara for capital goods: shops for wealthier customers (usually expatriates). They sell fridges, washing machines, microwave ovens, whatever you want, and they would certainly not be there if there were no demand. There *are* houses with tap water, shower, inside toilet, air-conditioning. But they are very few, and I don't know so much about them. There live expatriates and a few rich Solomon Islanders.

And just as Swedes appreciate natural tropical plants, which they don't have, then Solomon Islanders appreciate artificial silk or plastic flowers, which *they* don't have. Real flowers are seen as 'rubbish'. Thus, our veranda is decorated with hanging pots of silk flowers, while torch ginger, strelitzia (bird-of-paradise) and heliconia grow in abundance outside the door.

One decoration, which I have not seen anywhere outside Solomon Islands, is some kind of mobile – not the one used for calling, but a hanging ornament – made of strings and folded plastic strips from colourful noodle or biscuit packets. Some make pompoms and tassels of red, white and blue plastic bags. There is obviously no limit to human creativity and the desire for colour and joy. The silk flowers and the mobiles dance in the cool breeze.

Koa Hill and its inhabitants

I look eastward over the front yard and see the neighbouring house where Robert's brother Jimmy is living, their kitchen and the pig pen. Jimmy's household constantly varies. In the beginning, his wife Lamaa was living there with their youngest child Andrew and the grandson Pati, two boys around 10-12 years old. Then Lamaa went to the home village and fetched the seven-year-old granddaughter Rosie, Pati's sister, and the two-year-old grandson Small Tome. They stayed for half a year. Then everybody went back home, and then came Jimmy's and Lamaa's eldest son Black Tome. (He is called so because he is unusually dark-skinned.) Now relatives come and go, stay for a few weeks or months, go back and are substituted by new. Some of them stay with us.

Everybody in Jimmy's household is Kwaio and speak of course Kwaio together.

It is very close between the two houses, two meters at most. The building style results in many holes and apertures in the walls. It is so poorly isolated that Robert and I, when we want to speak about something private, must whisper *plus* turn on the radio. Also, in our love life, we must be as quiet as mice. It felt a bit strange in the beginning, but it certainly brings a piquant of spice into it.

The whole of Robert's family has accepted me warmly and un-reservedly. Even the oldest patriarch came to inspect me: I think I passed the test. They took me into their community without being pushy.

One house a little further away is owned by our relative, a man named Stanley. He doesn't live there himself but rents it out: right now to two Kwara'ae sisters. One of them works at an internet café. Even farther along lives an older man with his second wife, their common daughter and the wife's daughter from her first marriage.

The man made a scandal when he, as a grey-haired widower, met this new woman and she got pregnant. His adult children were raging; he had dishonoured their mother's memory, etc. If he didn't want to live alone, he could move in with some of the children, they reasoned. The son had even planned his grave at the side of their mother. But at the same time, they were quite impressed that the old man was still 'able'. The 'old man' neither wanted to move to the children nor plan his grave. He wanted to marry this new woman; he could afford to pay the bride price, and so it happened, and a little girl was born. The man is very touching when he is carrying the baby. *Daddy luk osem granny*, he says. 'Daddy looks like a grandfather.' His adult children have now accepted it, albeit with reservations.

The man told his story. At the age of 13, his marriage was arranged with a woman of 35. They lived their life and had three children, but as may be expected, she died before him. But instead of accepting a life as a widower, he wanted more out of life. And then he met this new woman, and a baby was conceived.

Yet another house up the hillside is inhabited by Filemon and Susan, their four children and Susan's father. Filemon is from Isabel Province and Susan is half Isabel and half Kwaio. Susan's fun and humorous father unluckily suffered a stroke and was paralysed, so he returned to Isabel. The main reason was that it was too complicated for him to climb down to the toilet.

This little settlement of four houses is the last outpost of Koa Hill. The houses are situated some distance from the river in a very nice and airy environment. Coconut palms, pawpaw, banana, flame trees, banyan, frangipani, strelitzia, heliconia and torch ginger all grow here. You may call it Upper Koa Hill. Down by the river and closer to Chinatown is Lower Koa Hill, with a conglomeration of houses and the ground covered with mud and a few bushes. The area is very densely populated, and some might call it a slum. But they are fortunate to have both electricity and running water from communal taps.

There is yet another house westward, where Cathy lives with her family: husband, two daughters and the husband's sister. But this house is a part of Tuvaruhu district. The border between Koa Hill and Tuvaruhu runs exactly along the ditch between our house and Cathy's. Cathy is from Guadalcanal and her husband is Kwara'ae from Malaita. They speak Pijin with each other and with us. His sister Helen sells vegetables at the market. The two daughters go to school. Cathy is an industrious woman and runs a 'canteen', a microscopic store with sugar, salt, tayio, rice, biscuits. The family are Seventh-day Adventists (SDA) and keep Sabbath on Saturdays, and then the canteen is closed. Every morning (that is, except Saturdays) Cathy is baking and selling *ring cakes*, the Pijin word for doughnuts. It is so cosy to sit munching warm doughnuts in the chilly (well...) morning. 'Chilly' is everything under 25°C.

The temperature is amazingly even over the year; 31-33 degrees C at day and 24-25 at night.

These five houses in Upper Koa Hill form a unit. Robert is one of the few who has registered his piece of land at the Ministry of Lands, Housing and Survey. A land tenancy costs $100 a year, too expensive according to most settlers, who ignore this payment. Those inhabitants just select a piece of land and build a house there. The town is growing uncontrollably, and the authorities can, if they want to set an example, let bulldozers pull down every unregistered house. But not ours.

And everybody lives on a 'grassroots' level.

Residence permit

So far, for my first stay in Solomon Islands, I had only needed a tourist visa for three months. When those months were over, I took a flight to another country, and at my return, I could start from the beginning with three new months. But now I had neither time nor money for such adventures. I was actually going to live here!! I had to apply for a residence permit, a 'long-time visa'.

I had some sweaty trips to the Ministry of Commerce, Industries, Labour and Immigration, standing for hours in long queues. The general requirements are:

- a Police Certificate from the country of origin;
- a Medical Clearance from Solomon Islands;
- a bank account with a sum corresponding to a single airfare to the country of origin in case of deportation;
- a proof that the applicant can support her- or himself eco nomically (I wasn't yet married then. When somebody is married to a Solomon Islander, the spouse must guarantee economic support);
- a receipt of paid application fee;
- two photos;
- a cover letter.

At last, every requirement was fulfilled, and I gave them all the papers they wanted plus my passport.

'You can pick up your passport tomorrow,' they said.

So efficient! But the next day the decision-maker wasn't there, nor the following day. The third day there was a power-cut, and they could not open the computers, etc. I could only smile and come back the next day, and the next...

This is almost always the way it is when making contact with authorities, banks and other institutions. But usually after one or two weeks, it turns out to be okay. One just has to be mentally prepared.

Now I had my residence permit, valid for two years. How proud I was! I used it for the first time at Heathrow Airport in London when checking in to Honiara via Los Angeles and Nadi.

'Where is your return ticket?' asked the man behind the desk.

'Return to what?' I played a fool although I knew the answer.

'Your ticket back home,' he answered patiently.

'Oh no. I'm not coming back. *Solomon Islands is my home!*'

'Hmm. But then you must have a residence permit.'

'Of course,' I said and proudly drew out the precious paper.

And what a feeling it was, on arrival at Henderson International Airport in Honiara, to go directly to the queue for 'Residents'. How I had been looking forward to that! But since that queue was much shorter, they unfortunately put together the two queues and mixed us all together, and I could not show off my new status!

Daily life

I am sitting in the door to our house. Outdoors, life is awakening. It is six o'clock. The sun is just rising, which the roosters have already found out. The pigs and the children are hungry, which they are loudly letting the neighbourhood know. One neighbour thinks it is the perfect time to start working on his house. The hammering is echoing. A church bell far away is calling for the morning service. The duties of the day can begin.

For my part, they consist of washing yesterday's dishes in a bucket. The water comes from a pipe out of the hillside, only a few meters from the house. A very nice duty! The sun is shining, the water is glittering, mini-crabs are skittering around.

The next 'must' is to fetch water. I fill up empty mineral water bottles from another pipe some meters farther away, a pipe from deep inside the mountain with fresh drinking water. We normally use four to six bottles of 1½ litres per day for drinking and cooking, that is six to nine litres in total.

The breakfast consists either of leftovers from the previous day, for example fish casserole with rice or vegetable casserole with kumara, or of biscuits, or of Cathy's delicious doughnuts. The popular Coffeemix – instant coffee, milk powder and sugar – in hot water gives you a tasty drink. Because of the English colonial history, this drink is called *ti*, 'tea'. I have tried to introduce the word *kofi*, 'coffee' without any success, since it is confused with *kofi*, 'cough'.

Managing a household is somewhat time-consuming. Peeling kumara, washing rice, cleaning fish, chopping vegetables, grating coconuts to coconut milk. Going to the market. There we buy loads of fresh food, and since we have no fridge, as previously mentioned, we must go shopping almost every day. We buy staple food in some of the innumerable Chinese stores in Point Cruz or in Chinatown, preferably in wholesale amounts, which is cheaper. Around the house we grow bananas, coconuts and pawpaw of our own.

Photo 11

Another 'must', but not every day, is laundry. It is done by hand in cold water, also from the pipe from the hillside. You can soak the clothes in advance and thus let the water become heated by the sun. I wash in a bucket and rinse in running water. The clothes are, of course, hung outdoors. If there is sunshine, they will dry in no time. But I have to be observant – the weather may change fast, from a cloudless sky to lead-grey in a few minutes. Then I have to run and collect the clothes before the first raindrops fall.

From that same pipe, I take my shower, two-three times a day, wearing a lavalava. First thing in the morning, then maybe in the daytime when I come back from town and the body is boiling, and finally in the evening before sleep. This evening-shower is especially lovely, to wash away the stickiness of the day and enjoy the humid coolness of the velvet night.

The toilet is built over a stream almost down by the river and shared by four households. In the doorway there is a black plastic sack, which we hang fast on a nail when we go inside. Sometimes somebody forgets to shut the sack when they go inside; alternatively they shut it when they leave. So in doubtful cases you take some gravel and throw on the walls. If somebody shouts inside ('ôy' for men, 'ey' for women), you sit down on the fallen palm trunk and wait. If nobody shouts, you step inside. There, some planks are laid across the stream, and there you crouch. The products go straight down in the stream and then out in the river. Not everyone can afford toilet paper, and here you can study the alternatives: leaves, sticks, newspapers, the children's school notes...

Robert used to work as a bus driver for RAMSI. He worked in shifts, something which affected our daily routines. One week was the morning shift. Then he got up at half past four, while I kept sleeping. He had lunch at his job, and I made a simple breakfast and lunch for myself. On his return, we had more time and interest to spend on dinner. The other week was the evening shift. On those shifts we had a looong breakfast, kept chatting and doing different things in the house until he left. When he returned at midnight, we ate something small and went to bed.

My own doings consist of household work and of writing, for example this book. The power supply for the laptop is working at last, after what seemed like never-ending problems. Almost every day I go to town to do shopping or other errands. You can either go by minibus or by foot. Koa Hill is a settlement close to the inner city, Point Cruz. It takes half an hour or so to walk there. In the beginning, when I walked fast like a European, it took 20 minutes. Now I walk like an islander, slowly, with all the time in the world. I usually walk there and take the bus back, my arms heavy with shopping bags.

At the market

Honiara Central Market is an experience in itself with its displays of food, its colours and its smells. Heaps of white, pink, red and purple kumara lie on the ground and other root crops: *cassava, taro, idu, pana*, yam. On the tables, mountains of leafy greens are piled up. They are generally called *kabis*, although not everything is cabbage. It might be *kasume* (sweet fern), Chinese cabbage, *kankun* (water spinach, a kind of edible bindweed), taro leaves, pumpkin leaves... Solomon Islands is 'the land of beautiful leafy vegetables'. The vegetarian's paradise!

Then there are white-green shallots, light yellow corn, green string beans, orange pumpkins, white cucumbers, purple eggplants, greyish-green *ko'a* (mangrove fruit), conveniently ready-grated, green capsicum, red tomatoes. The two last-mentioned probably don't enjoy the climate; they are very small. Regular onions and garlic are imported and have the advantage of being quite long-lasting. Kabis and shallots droop in one day.

The market in Honiara is the first market of all I have visited in the Pacific – Samoa, Tonga, Tahiti, Cook Islands, Vanuatu, New Caledonia and Fiji – where *fruit* seems to play a role and is counted as food. In the other countries, people apparently don't consider fruit as real food but more as an expensive luxury for the tourists, alternatively food for pigs.

'Pawpaw is for pigs and tourists,' they say in Tonga. In Samoa you can only buy pineapple in tins. In Fiji I found it almost impossible to buy green coconuts. It is one of the myths about the Pacific that it is loaded with fruit. In Sweden, a dairy has named their fruit yoghurts 'Samoa' and 'Fiji'. Ha-ha-ha. If only they knew.

But here at the market in Honiara, the stalls are heavy with fruit, and cheap it is: pawpaw, mango, pineapple, five-corner, *litchi*, *jackfruit*, *java-apple*, *guava*, *inkori* and enormous amounts of bananas. Watermelon is surprisingly expensive, though. Young green coconuts can be consumed on the spot. The vendor opens it, and then you drink the coconut water inside – a green coconut can give up to half a litre of water.

Photo 12

They also sell dry brown coconuts, important for grating and cooking. side by side with imported Fanta. Consumed by the locals, that is to say. Everywhere else in the Pacific, coconuts have only been sold for tourists. But here there are hardly any tourists; all this splendour is for the country's own inhabitants.

Back to the market. At the fish section there are heaps of tuna: small ones at 20-30 cm and big whoppers at a half to one metre. The vendors are whisking away the flies and sprinkling water over the fish. In cooler boxes you can see reef fish in bright colours and on the ground edible shellfish and crabs. Meat, on the other hand, is rare. Fresh chicken and sometimes a pig cut in big pieces can be seen in the cooler boxes, but there are no fly-infested animal carcases like those that can be seen hanging in many other countries.

There is a small area with cooked food, for example fish and chips, or motu-baked fish with rice, or pudding made of grated cassava and banana. Unfortunately, there is no place to sit down and eat. The market in Port Vila in Vanuatu has a whole little restaurant section with tables and chairsbut not the market in Honiara. Finally, there is a little handicraft section with jewellery: gorgeous jewellery made of the traditional shell money from Langa Langa, Malaita.

PRICE EXAMPLES 2 2020, SBD	
Kumara $10/heap	Five-corner $0.50-1
Kabis $5-10/parcel	Watermelon $15-50
Pawpaw $3-10	Banana $5-15/bunch
Mango $1-5	Young green coconut $3-5
Pineapple $5-20	Dry brown coconut $1-3

On Saturdays there is a section with flowers of extravagant and sparkling colours. They are sold mostly for large events and jubilees and to restaurants, hotels and banks.

Most of the vendors are women, and many of them bring their babies. They, that is the babies, crawl around in the vegetable waste or lie at their mother's breast. And the vendors are *quiet*. Nobody shouts out their goods, and most important of all, nobody cares that I, as the only 'White', am there. Nobody chases me, trying to force me to buy their goods, which is so common in many countries. (This alone could be sufficient reason to choose this country to live in!) Occasionally, somebody might point out their heaps just for me and say humbly 'nice bananas' or 'five dollars'. It is a very pleasant and calm atmosphere. You take what you want, put it in your shopping bag and pay. No haggling, always the correct change and a smile. But many times, the vendor has no change and must go and borrow from somebody else.

The buses back to Koa Hill depart from Chinatown. They are small rickety minibuses with 12 seats. There is no gangway in the middle, so if somebody in the rear wants to get off, everybody must get off first. And then they must get on again. No sour faces. A ride costs $3, which is collected by a bus conductor. He calls out the bus stops, and when you want to get off, you whistle a mild 'sss'.

It is fun and exciting to stroll about town and do window-shopping and enjoy the street life, but then it is so nice to come home to Koa Hill again. Here it is quiet and peaceful. Sometimes some music can be heard from a radio or CD player. Melanesian reggae.

Pets

Here, islanders don't have any pets exactly in the European sense – well, maybe parrots. Dogs and cats may exist; they are not ill-treated by their owners, but they are not cuddled with either, and nobody wants to touch them – they are full of fleas. There are no hordes of aggressive stray dogs like those you can see in many parts of the world. Dogs and cats are generally well kept, but it doesn't mean that they live free from risks. Somebody who gets annoyed at somebody else's dog can kill it without any hesitation.

We have a dog for security, a cat for rats and a parrot for pleasure. We have poor imaginations when it comes to names. The dog is named Puppy (even though he is an adult), the cat Pussy and the parrot Kilori (which means 'parrot' in Kwaio). Before, we had two dogs. But one day we found one of them dead, killed by somebody, who clearly had got annoyed. We have also had a number of cats and found them dead, too, bitten by dogs. 'The dog on the cat, the cat on the rat...'

Puppy was severely cut recently with a knife by an evil man. There is a veterinarian in Honiara, but it was impossible to get the dog to him for stitches. He, that is the dog, hates water and refused to go on board the raft across the river to the main road. So we gave him a half-dose of antibiotic for humans, which you can buy at the pharmacy without a prescription, and mixed it in his food, and he survived.

Pussy is still a kitten who is not very useful yet, but he is cute and fun and gets on with the dog. He has good hunting instincts, and trains on the geckos that skitter in and out.

Kilori is very beautiful, with a red body, green wings with blue spots, a yellow neck and a black head. We bought her at the market in Robert's village for $20. She had been caught in the jungle, where they live in abundance. At the market here in Honiara, they cost $100-150. Kilori can talk, say her name and 'kaikai'; she can twitter, whistle and laugh. She is chained to a *loia cane* (kind of thin cane, used for weaving), which is tied between our house and a tree. She loves sitting under the tree, in rain and in sunshine. The beauty of the red body against the green tree is striking.

The parrot was my birthday present from Robert. Normally birthdays are not celebrated in Solomon Islands, since the islanders in general don't know when they are born. But I know, and I gave a hint to Robert that in Sweden, people give presents on someone's birthday. Having a parrot has been my dream, ever since I decided to immigrate here. But Pussy and Kilori do row.

Pigs

I am sitting on my favourite stone by the river and watching the sunset. Then the air is shattered by a horrible sound from the pig pen across the river. Our neighbour is slaughtering his pig on the spot; the pig is writhing and screaming in angst and pain. Terrified, I follow the bloody spectacle, which goes on for an eternity. But there will be an end in only one way; at last the horrible screaming ceases, and the lifeless body is carried away. Ill at ease, I am thinking that I will never eat meat again. But I know that I will do it again, for I am a hypocrite and can accept eating a killed animal, as long as I don't have to kill it myself.

Pigs are seen as food for tomorrow and nothing else. People don't seem to care about the wellbeing of the animal.

In the beginning, we, too, had pigs. First, we had a sow which later had five cute, cute piglets. They grew fast, and after some time they were a metre long and not cute at all. How six pigs can eat and shit! Our constant worry was how to get feed for them. This is no problem in the villages, as I remember, too, from my childhood in Sweden. Pigs simply get potato skin and other waste food. But here in town, where all food must be bought expensively, here it will not work. Potato skin must be cooked, which demands expensive firewood or gas. The processed pigs' feed, 'Millrun', must be bought in 40 kg sacks. And the food is always out of stock; 'will come on Saturday', and today is Tuesday, and soon the pigs will be hungry. In those cases, we (or Robert, actually) must go to the market and beg for waste fruit or young coconut shells and dig out the fruit meat. But for this, one needs large quantities. Or we can sacrifice our own pawpaw, but how long will that last?

Apart from this, it was a drudgery to keep the pen clean. For some time, we (or I, actually) were leading water through a hose to a drum. But when that arrangement broke down, I had to scoop with a bucket, two or three times a day.

The pigs demanded constant care, and we began to tire. The mother-sow was sold first, as well as two piglets. The last straw was a conflict with a neighbour. His boar was the father of the piglets. Tradition holds that the owner of the father-boar should be given one new-born piglet. But this neighbour refrained.

Kipim, 'Keep it,' he said.

Later, when the piglet was almost adult and had cost us lots of food, time and trouble, *then* he wanted it. The fuss went on for an eternity, until Robert lost his patience and decided to slaughter it on the spot, 'so there wouldn't be anything left to fuss about'.

I was worried that I would have to be active during the slaughter, but this is the duty of the men. Instead, I went away with my hands over my ears, as well as Lamaa, my sister-in-law. Surprisingly, as she is a sturdy farmer and used to those things.

Mi sori lo pik, 'I feel sorry for the pig', she said.

This killing, however, was over much faster than the scene on the other side of the river. After a well-aimed knife stab in the heart, there was a deafening silence.

The slaughter record was set by a veterinarian from Malaita. He was so skilful that the pig didn't even notice it.

There was a feast for everybody in Upper Koa Hill, except for the few Seventh-day Adventists, who don't eat pork. The pig was cut in large pieces, and the meat was sold to the five households. The meat had, of course, to be taken care of immediately; nobody else has a fridge either. What was not fried or motu-baked was immediately cut in small pieces and put in hollow bamboo canes, which were laid in the fire. Such bamboo-cooked meat can, if then reheated, last for some days. I told my relatives that the Swedes used to put the meat in salt, which they found interesting. Sweden has, by the way, fridge temperature outdoors almost all the year.

And then the two remaining piglets were sold, and we were free. Now we have been thinking about breeding chickens. It would be nice to nurture them and have eggs. But with new animals, it will surely mean the same jobs again.

Water and culture

Life in Solomon Islands consists of a fine net of relations, rules and considerations; all that is called 'culture'. A lot of it circles around water and purity. The Pacific islanders must be the cleanest people in the world, who preferably take a shower two or three times a day. *If they have access to water and soap.* The smell inside stores and buses tells that this is not always the case.

Free running drinking water is an incredible luxury, not shared by many areas in Honiara, even less in Solomon Islands, even less in the Pacific. It is a paradox that the islands in the Pacific Ocean suffer from a lack of water. Fresh water. While salt is imported.

Almost all the neighbourhoods in Honiara have public tap water from Solomon Islands Water Authority (SIWA), but it costs money, and the water is often off. The taps are placed outdoors, few and far between, and some people have to walk quite a long way. Water indoors is very unusual. The tap water is drinkable but not very tasty. There is mineral water in the stores, $5-10 for 1½ litres.

Out in the villages there are, at best, pipes from dams, or the village has bought a rainwater tank for several thousand dollars, or the village has no water at all. The villagers may have to walk or paddle for kilometres to refill from a tap in more fortunate villages, or from a river or from a waterfall.

But Koa Hill has the best water provision in the whole of Honiara, with running fresh water in small underground streams from the mountain. With this wonderful gift, we fill our bottles and jerrycans in pure delight.

Four pipes serve five households; that is, around 30 persons. In the morning a queue forms. Then you sit down on the fallen palm and chat. Anyone bringing a big bucket of laundry at six o'clock in the morning, when breakfast has to be cooked and everyone wants a shower before going to school or work, won't be popular. On the other hand, it is okay to jump the queue if somebody is in a hurry. One morning, when I was having a shower, wrapped in a lavalava, but still..., a woman brought a kettle.

'Excuse me,' she said, 'I just want to take some water.' And of course, she could.

Privacy is almost non-existent. You have to take a shower in your clothes or at least in a lavalava, in front of everyone. But if somebody of the opposite sex is washing their private parts, it is appropriate to look away.

To take a shower under running water, or bathe in a river or a waterfall, or bathe in a bath tub are all known by the same word in Pijin: 'swim'. People do it in order to get clean. To swim in the sea is unusual. Children may play and splash in the sea but not adults, even if they know how to swim. The prevalent view is that the sea is a workplace and a place for transport, not a playground. The lukewarm and sultry salt water is hardly refreshing, and it might cause itchiness and skin irritations. Water activities like snorkelling and diving are met by a lack of under-standing from the locals; it is something for tourists. Fish is for eating, not for watching.

A memory: Robert and I were in London Zoo Aquarium some years later. Everybody who entered the tropical room exclaimed: 'Oooh, look at those fish! They are so beautiful!' When Robert entered, he ex-claimed: 'Oooh, look at those fish! They are so *tasty*!'

But back to Koa Hill. Sometimes there are arguments about the waterpipes, and it is mostly between the Kwaio and non-Kwaio. The Kwaio have strict, almost ritualistic, rules for purity.

There is water running out of pipes from inside the mountain. The highest spring suits almost everything: cooking, dishwashing, laundry and personal hygiene. Maybe not for drinking water, as the spring is shallow and the water may contain mud after rain. The waste water from there goes to the second spring. It is not well frequented. Needless to say, you won't take water for cooking or dishwashing from any water that people have showered in. *Rabis wata*, 'rubbish water', it is called. But you can splash your feet, or take water to clean the pig pen. The third spring is suitable for drinking water, since it comes from deep inside the mountain. It used to be surrounded with a sackcloth and therefore preferred for personal hygiene. But for some reason. the sackcloth was taken away, and nobody has put up another one. Under the third spring, the water from the two first springs flows into one and runs down to the toilet, from where it flushes its various products out into the river. The fourth spring is independent of the other three. It has its own inflow and own drain. It is not suitable for drinking water, as it is shallow, but good for everything else: for cooking, for dishwashing and for personal hygiene.

Under the first and third springs there are petrol drums to collect the water. These must be kept absolutely clean, both from soap and from dirt. One morning, a not-so-bright Kwara'ae woman had filled the drum with dirty clothes, even underwear, and the Kwaio hit the ceiling in disgust. The drum was polluted forever and could never be used again. Robert overturned the drum with its contents and threw it all into the river, where it gurgled away in the brown water. All the while scolding the guilty woman.

Orthodox Kwaio cannot imagine dishwashing at the third spring. In the beginning I did not understand the problem. The water in the third spring is so clean; it comes from deep inside the mountain and is good enough to drink. It is not polluted by anything. But the question here is not *from where* the water comes but *where* it goes. It goes down to the toilet. And here is where the Kwaio culture comes in.

Since time immemorial, the Kwaio have a deep respect for food. There is hardly any waste; everything is used. But something, however, is always left over, be it grains of rice, crumbs, fishbones. That is why, in traditional villages, they eat sitting close to the fire, so these small leftovers can be consumed immediately by the fire and not be polluted. And food deserves a better fate than to be flushed down with toilet water. That is lacking in respect and absolutely taboo. Among the hidden people, it is a serious offence. The guilty must sacrifice at least one pig; otherwise the spirits will make something dreadful happen to them. The Christian Kwaio, too, take this seriously. It is simply a part of the Kwaio culture.

The cheerful radio meteorologist promised 'a nice day for washing and hanging your clothes'. The sun was frying, there was a slight breeze. It was indeed a lovely day. It sounded so pleasant that I told a woman from New Zealand. She snorted,

'How can you say washing is *nice*?'

But come on, all of us must wash; you just have to accept it (unless you have servants). If you can't find joy in your everyday doings, then where? In eternal play and entertainment?

Well, anyway, I think that it is nice to wash clothes in the fresh water from the mountain. The water is certainly always cold, but it works. I am using a bucket, the water is glittering in the sun and the washing powder, imported from Malaysia, smells nice. Rough textiles are brushed energetically. Then the clothes are hung from a line in the sun.

This is exactly what is nice. What a joy, compared to musty electric tumble-driers or drying cabinets. If it is a nice day, as the meteorologist said it would be, the laundry will be dry in no time. If it is raining, the laundry is hung under the house or on the veranda, but then it takes longer to dry, of course.

In principle, everybody washes their own clothes. The woman washes hers and the man his, especially clothes under-the-waist, and underwear. A woman can wash her husband's clothes but no other man's. A man can wash his wife's clothes, as long as nobody is looking. But definitely not another woman's. Women can wash for each other and men for each other. A woman can borrow the towel of another woman and a man of another man. But not across the gender borders. A married man can borrow a young boy's towel, but a young boy cannot borrow a married man's towel (since it is 'polluted'), etc...etc...

Photo 13

The battle about the energy

For some time, we had electricity, but it was suddenly closed down, although I didn't really understand why. So now, the energy source of the day is solar panels. Ben, a relative who is an electrician, offered to sell us a second-hand 80-watt panel for $5,000. Expensive, but in the stores, they would cost much more, so we made a deal. In addition, Ben would help us to install it. Filemon, our neighbour and an electrician too, wrote a long list of all accessories we had to buy. Ben brought his panel, Robert climbed up on the roof and fastened it. Ben installed cables, controller, inverter and whatever all was called, and then we tested the electric cooker from Sweden. All the fuses burned in a flash.

Now followed some tragi-comical months, which we spent in traffic shuttling between stores selling panels, stores selling controllers and stores selling inverters. (No store sold it all together.) They all gave different advice. A kind Chinese store owner told us that we could forget about cooking with solar energy. Changing of temperature, e.g., heating or cooling, is extremely power consuming. He advised us to cook with gas. If you want to look at it positively, you can say that we *learned a lot about solar panels and electricity*. Had we known from the beginning what we know now, we would have acted differently and saved thousands of dollars.

I will not bore you, reader, with details. In the end we are sitting here with one gas bottle for cooking, two solar panels and three batteries: one for lights, one for charging of mobiles, laptops and electric razors and one for spare. ('Had we known...' etc.) After a cloudy day, the power does not last the whole evening. And we can only use the DVD player and the trendy TV set for a few hours, enough for a movie.

Later on, however, the technology developed, and the stores started to sell complete solar packets with everything included. Cheaper and childishly simple. ('Had we known...' etc.)

Guadalcanal and war movies

There are some geographical names which are associated with fear, depending on what one has heard about them at a certain time. In some cases, the time is gone, but the feeling remains. Auschwitz is such a name. Phnom Penh is another. Mekong, the river where dead bodies were floating during the Indochina war. Rwanda, the site of the improbable civil war. And then Guadalcanal.

Guadalcanal is the main island in Solomon Islands, the largest one and the site for the capital Honiara. Seen from Honiara the inner parts of the island seem inaccessible. Since the island has no roads except a single one on the north coast, it seems to be beyond reach, daunting and hostile.

One sunny and peaceful day Lamaa and I were busy chopping down dry banana leaves in the yard of our houses in Guadalcanal. We were surrounded by greenery; it looked like a wild jungle, although it was an urban area. We were chopping, the sweat was pouring, we enjoyed the fresh smell from the greenery and took a short break. Then we heard it.

The silence was broken by a threatening rumble above us, a motor sound. Our faces were turned towards the sky, and then we saw it: the silver bird. A helicopter was circling over our houses, the rotor blades flapping. We were standing there in Guadalcanal's jungle, two human beings living in peace, and then came an unknown element and threatened our existence. What was it doing here; why did it disturb the peace in our jungle? Was I in a war movie? Goosebumps rose.

The Thin Red Line came to my mind – the movie about the Battle of Guadalcanal, which is horrible but at the same time pacifistic, since it displays warfare as an absolute impossibility.

It was on Guadalcanal that a major World War II battle took place between the Japanese and Allied Forces. The Battle of Guadalcanal 1942-1943 was a critical turning point, which strongly contributed to the victory of the Allied Forces and eventually to the end of the war. The warfare resulted in severe damage for Guadalcanal and for the island of New Georgia, and the inhabitants there had to, without actually having anything to do with this thing, see their country being bombed to Swiss cheese. The by-then capital Tulagi was reduced to rubble, and Honiara became the new capital.

But what was the helicopter actually doing there? The truth is that our suburb is situated near the Parliament, and there was a session going on there, and the helicopter was a Solomon police helicopter. Like in a time tunnel I was taken back to the present. We went on chopping.

Palm felling

The coconut palm in the yard had been a source of annoyance for a long time. Under its crown, a bunch of lethal yellow missiles were hanging, which could be dropped at any time on innocent passers-by. Falling coconuts are a common cause of death in the tropics! When it also shaded our solar panel on the roof, its fate was sealed: The palm must go! Even though I hit the roof over this assault of a sacred tree.

First of all, a young man climbed up the trunk. Someone had cut steps in the trunk, and he tied a rag around his feet, so that was easily done. Up there, he began to chop down the coconuts with his bush knife. The nuts flew in all directions; many of them broke when they hit the ground, and the coconut water sprayed all over. The nuts were collected. The broken ones were put for compost or for firewood. The rest were put under the house to be enjoyed as a drink another day. All the coconuts were still in the young stage, when there is plenty of water inside, and the meat is still soft and jelly-like. Then the man chopped off most of the branches. They were put aside to be woven into baskets and brooms.

This was just the beginning. A rope was needed, a long rope. The rope for the raft across the river was 25 meters and too short. Robert remembered the 50-meter-long electric cables, which had been taken out when the electricity was closed down. Another man hurried up and tied the cable in the palm crown, and the palm was pulled in the direction where it would cause the least damage. Still, the toilet was in the danger zone. The women took away the children, while the men began cutting with an axe and started pulling, pulling. After an amazingly short time, the trunk broke and fell with a terrible bang. Cats, dogs and hens ran in all directions. See how brittle a coconut palm is; a tree would have taken an eternity to fell. Well done; the toilet was saved with ten centimetres' margin, and as for the plants in the yard, only one banana plant was crushed. The trunk was cut up in three pieces; two pieces became a bridge across the stream, and one piece became an excellent 'story bench' in the yard. A 'story bench' is a bench where you sit *story* 'chatting' about more or less true stories.

Bugs and other annoyances

I know that there are more insects in the world than mammals and birds and fish combined. For each human being there are 200 million insects. But I didn't know that they all must be *around me*. Fierce mosquitoes (malaria-carrying even), gnats, horseflies, fleas, lice, cockroaches, stag beetles, black flies, blue flies, yellow flies, big orange coconut ants, red ants that bite, black ants that don't bite – this is just the beginning. They bite and sting and leave – at best – big or small red dots, which soon disappear or – at worst – shivering and a rash or boils, which swell and itch up to two weeks. The most intense time for these bugs is dusk; I arm myself with spray, roll-on and mosquito coils. We sleep under mosquito net. I am *still* bitten!

My relatives laugh and say that 'Whites' have 'sweet blood'. They themselves are less affected. It cannot be the diet, since I eat the same food as they do. I have read somewhere that bugs are attracted to certain blood groups. I can swear it is *my* blood group (A-).

This is a paradise almost without snakes. A few poisonous (but not deadly) snakes, no scorpions, no poisonous spiders. Sharks and crocodiles, yes. Solomon Islands has one of the highest numbers of attacks by saltwater crocodiles in the world. And the number is increasing!

The new veranda

The old veranda was really decrepit, and we had to renovate it, before it fell down and caused an accident. All neighbours, relatives and friends who could were helping us, so it was done in no time. The roof and walls were pulled down, and the boards in the floor were torn up. A temporary veranda without a roof was made up, and a ladder was quickly erected, replacing the stairs, as easy as one, two, three. I could but admire these handy, skilful people.

Then we had to clean up the house. It became a farce. We took out everything to the temporary veranda, and then we (well, Robert) climbed up on the beams and swept away dust and spiderwebs, and then we put everything back again. Even though we have not much property and hardly any furniture, it still took some time. The next day we got a message from Honiara City Council that they would come and spray inside the house against malaria mosquitoes, and that we should take out everything. So we had to do it again, and then there was a tropical downpour, and the kitten had diarrhoea that Robert stepped in.

Sometimes Robert and I say 'Give me this something' when we both know what we mean but don't know the word in Pijin or English. But now he was only shouting 'Give me something', and since he was in another room it was not easy to know what he meant. 'It's on my foot!' he kept shouting...

Then we started to build the new veranda. It was fascinating to follow the process from beginning to end. Getting boards was not so fascinating. We went to a timber merchant, bought the boards and rented a truck for transport to the house. (Another option would have been to cut our own trees in the home village for free, but they had to be milled and freighted by ship to Honiara, so the cost would end up the same, and it would take weeks.) It was a bit adventurous to get the timber across the river on the raft, but we managed that, too.

After this, the walls and roof would be made of sago palm leaves. A kind neighbour let us, for $100, cut down branches from one of the 15-20-metre-tall sago palms on his plantation. Robert tied together some long stakes and attached a crooked bush knife at the top. This way he could, from the ground, cut down the branches. The leaflets were cut from the leaf stem, cleaned and tied into bundles with great skill and floated across the river. At our house, they were sewn up with thin loia cane to sheets of 2-3 metres long.

Sago palm looks like coconut palm but has larger leaves. When they are cut down, the leaves are intensely green, but after some days when they have dried, they become light brown. Laid in layers on top of each other they become totally rainproof. A group of men helped us to place the leaves to form walling and a roof. The leaves were skilfully tied with loia cane. Then we had among the most beautiful houses in the whole of Koa Hill.

Photo 14

The new veranda became a meeting point for our neighbourhood. The old one was so dark and gloomy, but this one is bright and airy with a lowrailing, over which you can stand philosophising and look out over the river. On the veranda many things are done. We cook and eat. Somebody brings her sewing machine; others plan a letter to some authority and type it on my laptop. I copy it to my flash drive and print at some internet café in town. We are one of the few households with a TV. We used to have nine TV channels, so we kept an eye both on the Georgia crisis and the Football World Cup in South Africa 2010. Now, unfortunately, Our Telekom has raised a tower just above our house, which interferes with the signal. So instead, we watch video on our TV or, after our travels abroad (see below), endless digital photos. Very few of our guests here have been abroad, and everybody is very interested.

Since the veranda is the public part of the house, anyone may come inside and have a seat – well, provided that we know them of course. For me in the beginning, it felt a little strange that neighbours and relatives just walked in and had a seat. Especially when I was busy with something; for example, writing this book. But I have got used to it. There is no choice, as *this is the core of Melanesian culture.* I was given the advice to shut myself up in the house and pretend to *sleep.* The inner house is, as we said, the private part, and sleeping is an acceptable way to withdraw. But sleep all day...?

I am sitting on the new veranda writing; the dog is sleeping on the stairs. Robert and Stanley are talking in soft Kwaio, Robert is busy with the remote control to the DVD player. In passing, he bawls at the neighbour children who are filching our pawpaw. The thermometer shows 34°C.

Time is running by so fast. I realize that when I receive emails from Sweden. It was just June, now it is December. It still happens from time to time that I am struck by a paralyzing fatigue due to all the new impressions. But otherwise, calm and harmony. This is the life I wanted to live, a quiet life in purity and simplicity in a tropical country. Soon it is Christmas.

Malaita

At sea

I was sitting on the lid of the cargo section, staring in front of me. I was not thinking,

Imagine – I am in my dream country at last. Imagine – me on board the cargo-passenger ship L C Dragon with my beloved Solomon Islanders around me. And reggae on the radio. What faces, what characters. What dynamics on this ship, what a vibrant activity, how I admire these people. But I could have thought this, because it was true.

I was not thinking,

Oh shit, how annoying and noisy people are, and what shrill voices the women have. And how crowded it is, and how hot from the engine room, and how it smells like petrol from there and like shit from the toilet. I am tired, deadly tired, 24 hours in this tub, I can't manage it. It was true, too.

I was thinking Nothing.

Drugged with seasick pills, I slept sprawled out on a sack of rice. The voyage took 31 hours, not 24. And surely, I could manage it.

We were going to spend Christmas in Robert's village Fousisigi, located in Sinaragu bay. There are no roads going there, no power lines, no telephone lines. But surely you can get there. You can either fly to Auki (30 minutes), or get there by cargo-passenger ship (6-13 hours) or take a speed boat (3-6 hours). From Auki you take a truck and sit on the tray (4 hours) across the north of Malaita to Atori, then take a motorboat (2 hours) to Sinaragu, and look! There lies Fousisigi like a jewel deep in the bay.

Yet another way is to fly to Atoifi, south of Atori, and continue by motorboat. Atoifi has an airstrip and a relatively large and well-kept hospital (with a striking lack of resources), a bank and some stores.

Whichever way you go, the toughest part is the last section by motorboat to the villages of Sinaragu. And to take a motorboat, you must have made an agreement with the skipper to be picked up, and you should bring your own petrol.

One last alternative is therefore the most popular one: a cargo-passenger ship directly from Honiara to Sinaragu (2-3 days). But the ship schedules are unreliable. They normally run every second week.

But sometimes the departure can be postponed a few days or a week or so. The reasons might be engine problems, overload, changing of route or 'political problems' (whatever that is) among the crew, engine problems again. But *if* you are finally on board, the crowd is incredible. On those trips you can bring all kinds of goods from Honiara that are needed in the village; mattresses, kerosene lamps, rice sacks, cases of noodles, bales of clothes for sale, petrol drums, building material like masonite, corrugated sheet metal and nails... Some live pigs are standing tethered on deck or lying down with all four legs tied to a pole.

Christmas is the longest leave in Solomon Islands, and everyone who can is going 'home', and 'home' is always the village where they are born and own land. People begin to talk about Christmas already in September. *Kolesap Christmas!* 'It is close to Christmas!' Shops and hotels in Honiara latch on with knick-knacks, Jingle Bells and plastic fir trees.

But now about the voyage. This was not my first trip to Sinaragu bay. The year before I had visited Gounabusu (see Part I), but it was my first visit in Fousisigi, and with my new relatives. So I boarded the *L C Dragon* together with Robert, Jimmy, Lamaa and hundreds of other passengers. *L C Dragon* was one of those crammed-full rust-buckets that you read about, noisy and dirty. I slept sometimes and vomited sometimes. It was night, and it was day and then night again. We were passing by harbours named Laualu, Manabu, Lagualu, Nakuano, Ata'a, Kwai and Atoifi.

After 31 hours we arrived at Sinaragu. The ship could not touch the shore but had to stay in the middle of the bay. From there, we were picked up by motorboats and dugout canoes and ferried to the shore.

Photo 15

East Kwaio

East Kwaio is situated on the east side of Malaita. The most well-known district is Sinaragu bay, with the surrounding villages Su'ubonu, Malo'u, the main village Gounabusu, Fousisigi, Gelebase, and many others.

Between the villages, people move by dugout canoes. Most villagers live along the narrow coastal area as well as in scattered villages in the mountains. The villagers make a living from agriculture on the mountainsides and from fishing. They practise crop rotation and slash-and-burn agriculture. The climate in East Kwaio is different from that in Honiara. The magnificent mountains attract rain, and it is *always* raining. It must have the world's highest rainfall rate. It is pouring for hours, and the village road is transformed into muddy puddles. The laundry never dries, etc.

Tourism has not really caught on, due to the difficult communications. Otherwise there is a lot to see and do here: take part of a living culture, enjoy waterfalls, go trekking in the rain forest to the hidden people, visit historically interesting sites like the places of William R. Bell's murder and Roger Keesing's urn. Some occasional tourist groups find their way here, however. And then some individual 'wild-brains'. Like me, the year before.

William R. Bell was a British District Officer who was assassinated in 1927 when trying to collect tax from the obstinate Kwaio. His murder (which was carried out by a few extremists without support of other Kwaio) led to a revenge massacre of the Kwaio, the Malaita massacre. The British administration was aided by North Malaitan police and volunteers, who burned villages, killed almost hundred innocent people, poisoned their crops and offended or destroyed cult objects. This is neither forgotten nor forgiven. The Kwaio have not yet received justice, and the question of compensation is still being discussed fruitlessly after almost 100 years.

Roger Keesing was a linguist and anthropologist established in Australia who lived with the Kwaio, learned their language and documented their culture. In addition to numerous anthropological publications, he also compiled a grammar and a dictionary of the Kwaio language. When he died in 1993, the urn with his ashes was taken to the hidden people, where it is still kept today. He has been accorded the status of an *andalo*, ancestral spirit. If his skull had been kept, it would no doubt have its given place in the skull house with the skulls of honoured ancestors and other dignitaries.

Fousisigi

Robert's village, Fousisigi, is situated in the middle of Sinaragu bay on a small strip of land by the sea, fringed by coconut palms and surrounded by green hills. Apart from the rocky beach, there is only around fifty metres of land which is flat. The shore line is extremely low, and there is a big difference between low and high tide. The village manages by the skin of its teeth during normal tide. But around three days per month, the high tide is extremely high, and then half of the village street is under water.

Photos 16-17

Above the shoreline the jungle encloses the little village, where almost all houses are made of bamboo and sago palm leaves. Above the village, the impressive mountains rise up. The steep slopes are cultivated with root crops, mostly kumara. After the gardens follows deep rain forest, and here live the hidden people. There are five hours of trekking on muddy paths to their first village. For tourists. They themselves jump sure-footedly down to the coast and back. Robert was born on the coast, but his parents come from the mountains.

Fousisigi has seven households with dwelling houses, separate kitchens and pig pens, and all the villagers are related. There is a large, permanent wooden house, which belongs to Jimmy and Lamaa. It was inhabited by the unmarried son Tome, the married son Firifaka with his wife Rubaka and their two children, the old Aunty Kwaleka and a 15-year-old niece Tuini. But since Tome has married, and Firifaka and Rubaka have had their third child, the two families have built their own little houses but with a common kitchen.

It is not very common to have three generations under the same roof. When the adult children marry, they build a new house when they can afford it (that is, afford *nails*, while trees, bamboo and sago palm grow free around the house). Alternatively, the young ones keep living in the first house, while the elderly build themselves a new, smaller one, a 'granny flat'. Still, the generations keep living close to each other.

While Jimmy is slim, Lamaa is sturdily built. So are their six children: five sons and one daughter. In the beginning, I could only distinguish the eldest and the youngest of the sons, while the three sons in the middle looked so much like each other that it took me an eternity to distinguish them (they are not triplets). Now I can do it most of the time, but as soon as any of them changes hair style or beard, I'm lost again.

Aunty Kwaleka is one of the few who doesn't know even a single word in Pijin, and my Kwaio is still poor. But funnily, it is with her I have the best contact. We simply like each other and can show it in many ways: with smiles, hand pressings, little snacks... She gives me a taro root she has roasted in the embers and scraped clean – I give her a sachet of Coffeemix. Aunty Kwaleka has never married, and now she is the rock when it comes to babysitting.

Aunty Kwaleka experienced the Malaita massacre, but she does not remember it. She was a toddler and had to be carried, while the family were escaping.

Photo 18

Farther down, just by the sea, live Pastor John's sister and his old mother in a permanent house. Pastor John used to live there, too.

However, his late father came to him in his sleep and warned of a tsunami, so John and his wife Rose decided to build a new house high on a hill. Henceforth, mean tongues laugh at him and call him 'John Tsunami'. But he who laughs last, laughs loudest!

The next building is the modest church. It has no walls and consists principally of roof and benches. But it is a sacred building, and the altar is decorated with fresh red hibiscus flowers. Beyond the church comes Uncle Pati and Aunty Joycelyn's little palm leaf house. It is poor and decrepit, but they are too old to renovate it. Uncle Pati has a glint in his eyes and speaks fluent Pijin and a little English. He asks me to take a photo of him and his Medal of bravery from World War II. Joycelyn is very small and thin and has the frizzy reddish-brown hair that is so common in Malaita. This precious little butterfly-like creature and Aunty Kwaleka are the oldest women in the village, both slim and sinewy. Both had their teeth dyed black, as the fashion prescribed when they were young. The teeth were polished with a black stone until they were black and shiny, to make them strong and beautiful. They are definitely strong; Aunty Kwaleka is almost 90, and she has all her teeth.

The nature around Fousisigi looks like the inside of a palm house in a botanical garden, a greenhouse for tropical indoor plants or a well-stocked florist's shop. The plants are those we see in pots in Sweden: small pots for private homes, big pots with expensive ornamental plants for open plan offices or public decoration: philodendron, monstera, hibiscus, orchids, silver aralia, fiddle leaf fig, callas, ficus, amaryllis, lilies, bird's nest bracken, ferns, angel's trumpet, dracaena, India-rubber tree, croton. Here, they grow like shrubs or bigger. Not to mention fruit: banana, pawpaw, mango, inkori and lots of others whose names I don't know.

Dishwashing, laundry and showers take place at four public taps with water from rivers in the mountains, collected into a dam. Fousisigi is one of the few villages with that kind of water supply. Therefore, people from other villages come in canoes and refill water in bottles and jerrycans. They also take the opportunity to wash clothes and to shower. Sometimes the taps are crowded, and the Fousisigi inhabitants can hardly get access themselves. Since the taps leak fiercely, or people forget to turn them off, or they cannot be turned off at all, the dam is emptied sometimes and the water is finished. Then, lemonish comments are muttered about the water consumers:

'*They* finish the water, when *we* need it.'

In Fousisigi, like everywhere else, the villagers shower in the full glare of the public, but in their clothes. Toilet business is done on the south shore for women and on the north shore for men, and then the tidal water comes and takes care of it all.

The pig pens are built on posts in the sea, so the waste can drop down into the water. Practical, but not exactly inviting for a swim there. Behind the clotheslines and behind the pig pens, yes, there is the lagoon.

At six o'clock, the darkness descends suddenly, like a coal sack around you. Very soon the coal sack is brightened by merry kerosene lamps and one or two solar lamps. Time for chatting on the upside-down canoe on the beach. A mild ukulele tinkle, and indeed, reggae from a keyboard – battery operated, of course. And the full moon emerges from behind the palms. The lagoon glistens in the moonshine; the evening is black velvet.

Friday market in Wa'ini

This market is the highlight of the week. Just at the sunrise, to this little green clearing covered with grass with the deep, deep green jungle around and above it, farmers and fishermen come from all over Sinaragu to sell their products. The canoes are tied at the beach. There are no tables or chairs; the vendors simply place their goods on canvases on the ground. It could be kabis, pumpkin, pineapple, banana, cooked food like pudding, grilled fish and pastries like pirogues, doughnuts and muffins. Two store owners from nearby villages display their assortment: noodles, tayio, sugar, salt, soap, pens, rubber bands, wicks for kerosene lamps... Some members of the hidden people have come down from the mountains and stay a bit for themselves. They sell betel nuts and tobacco, and with the cash, they buy modernities like knives, razors and matches.

Everyone in Fousisigi speaks Kwaio and, as a second language, Pijin, everyone but Aunty Kwaleka. But at the Friday market there are yet some persons, even youngsters, who only speak Kwaio. Luckily, I have learnt to ask *Ola pita?* 'How much?' Kwaio language has a full set of numerals, but interestingly, the speakers have nowadays adapted Pijin numerals. And they are the same as in English. Or the vendors answer with their fingers. So I do not need to go hungry from the Friday market.

The Kwaio have a long tradition of money-trading, as a contrast to swap-trading. Even before, when there were no banknotes or coins, they paid for goods or services with shell money.

The Friday market is the great information central. Men and women gather in groups and exchange 'information' (read: gossip). Agreements are concluded. Boys and girls check each other out. By around 9 a.m., the market is closed.

From Fousisigi to Wa'ini, you can either paddle in five minutes or – if low tide – walk a path in ten. Between Fousisigi and Wa'ini is Gwee'abe, which is the place William R. Bell was assassinated, and others with him. Some victims were buried there, but not Bell himself. The area around the graves was taken care of by Robert's father for many years but has now been forgotten, overgrown by the jungle.

Robert's father, the late Tome Arika, was a respected local leader and mediator. Before Independence, he functioned as a link between the British administration in Malaita and the Kwaio community. He was called Tome *Kalaka* ('Clerk') and used to carry a knapsack with his writing gears.

Photo 19

Christmas in Fousisigi

From having been backwoods most of the year, Fousisigi was now filled with people. They don't live permanently here but in the towns; in Auki or in Honiara. Everybody hates Honiara and regards Fousisigi as 'home'. Long before Christmas, they start talking about going 'home' and ask if I am going 'home', too. But for me, 'home' is synonymous with Koa Hill.

These urban relatives bring incredible pieces of property: solar panels, TV screens for video (TV coverage is missing) and mobile phones.

I was soon accepted as *niu missis blong Robert*, 'Robert's new wife'. Lamaa welcomed me, saying that we were one and the same family. We were not married then, the first Christmas, but if a couple live together, they are regarded as married.

That I existed and furthermore was 'White' was not any news. Here, news spreads even before it has happened, and this without telephones, internet or anything like that (but with the Friday market). Everyone had heard of me, wanted to meet me and greet me. The friendliness and the welcoming were overwhelming. I had brought some t-shirts and small solar lamps from Sweden, tayio, sugar, salt and lollies. In return, I received an unbelievably well-worked bag, a kastom basket.

Some members of the hidden people came down to the coast for a visit. And *they* had not heard about the *niu White missis* (Now how could they miss that new information?), so their eyes were glittering with sensation. A man said that *he* would never dare marry a 'White'. But the elders have Roger Keesing fresh in their memory and know that 'Whites' can respect Kwaio kastom.

What do they mean by kastom and what do I mean? For me, it is the same phenomenon that appears in Vanuatu, New Caledonia and Fiji, and by all means in many other parts of the world: manners and traditions, values and mentality, yes, everything that is called culture. The Kwaio (especially the hidden people's) culture is the very quintessence, the hard core, of Melanesian culture.

Sometimes I don't know if the Kwaio kastom is typical only for East Kwaio...or Malaita...or Solomon Islands...or Melanesia... Some features, e.g., of purity, I recognize among the Roma (Gypsy) culture, and very, very much is general for all mankind, just in higher or lower degrees in different parts of the world.

When I went for a visit to Sweden, my friends there collected money for Swedish football uniforms for the team in Fousisigi. Now they were to be inaugurated! There was a football tournament going on in the villages around Sinaragu. The players were very proud of the yellow shirts with the blue-and-yellow Swedish flag and the blue trousers. With those uniforms they would surely win! They kept training and training under Robert's guidance, and then they paddled to the host village of the tournament. Their uniforms were again admired and envied. No other team had such a fancy outfit. Fousisigi lost in a flash.

The following year there was a tournament for women's football, then a panpipe festival, then a school jubilee. Sinaragu is very dynamic!

Families in Melanesia are large. In our house with four bedrooms and one living room, there were around 20 persons staying: eight adults, six teenagers, four children and two babies. Temporary guests came and went. I also met Robert's other siblings. Previously, I had only met Jimmy. They are five: brother Jimmy, brother Pati, sister Abuka, Robert and then sister Abi.

For me there followed an easy-going existence which consisted of visits, food, sleep, more visits, more food, more sleep. That is to say, easy-going on my part. The women of the village are responsible for food. Almost every day they climbed to their gardens in the mountains to fetch kumara. And I developed my language skills.

At Christmas, the adults chat, the little cousins are up to mischief. People meet, slaughter pigs and eat. The main thing is that they come together. There are hardly any Christmas traditions, but worship in the little church is a must. People come paddling from surrounding villages. The congregations are not large, so the churches take turns holding services, and that year, for this important Christmas Day, it was Fousisigi's turn. I was personally welcomed and had to stand up and tell about myself. The service became an intense experience. They were playing guitar and singing – that was just the beginning; then followed testimonies about salvation, ecstasy, speaking in tongues, quaking, dancing, body movements that were clearly sexually influenced. But then the rest of the church, who were not quite that affected, began to squirm a little. (Dancing in general has sexual associations and is, anyway, improper.)

Around 92% of Solomon Islanders are Christian. The largest denominations are: Anglican Church of Melanesia, Roman Catholic Church, South Seas Evangelical Church, United Church and Seventh-day Adventist Church. Around 5% practise indigenous religion. Others include Jehovah's Witnesses, Mormons, Jews, Muslims, Baha'i and more.

At the end of the service, Pastor John asked for contributions to one small group of the parish, who had just left the hidden people in the mountains, converted to Christianity and settled on the coast. They had nothing. The contributions consisted of money, food (especially kumara) and clothes. Unprepared for this, I rushed to the house and fetched a 1-kg-packet of rice and a 20-dollar note, which I tried to hide in the heap of other contributions. Some of the gifts were well wrapped. It is not a good practice to show your gifts in public.

Late on Christmas Day, the whole village ate a huge, common supper in the yard, consisting of motu-baked pig, fish, kabis, kumara, cassava, rice and much more. The food was served on banana leaves on the ground.

Photo 20

Boxing Day, at midnight when everybody was asleep, I woke up to lovely singing voices. It was a small women's group who were paddling around singing *kerols*, 'carols'. That was gospel songs in Kwaio, Pijin and English, performed with joy. Delighted, all villagers woke up and went outdoors, and many left a small contribution in the form of food and money.

And around New Year, a group of youngsters came blowing and beating panpipes, and they were given food and money, too. Panpipes are traditionally built of bamboo canes, as previously mentioned. Well, it is supposed to be bamboo canes, but PVC plastic waterpipes are just as good. Some youngsters in one village filched the waterpipes intended for the school and built panpipes. What the school said is another story...

Nowadays panpipes of PVC are more frequent than those of bamboo; they give a better tune.

Village life

Strong sunshine after the night's rain. I'm sitting on the stairs of the house. The morning duties are done. Moderate activity in the village. In front of me a coconut palm, brim-full with nuts – I just need to tell a boy to climb and get one. But I don't. Instead, I study the surroundings. On the ground around the palm, some piglets are rooting. Out in the lagoon, a man is paddling a canoe. The idyll is total. Suddenly the silence is torn apart by a motorboat. Then, again, silence.

Somebody is asleep after the slaughter of a pig in the morning. Some are playing handball. Somebody is going to the pigs with a bucket of swill. A two-year-old is playing with a bush knife.

Somebody comes, as happy as a lark, carrying a plastic bag and shows me what he has been given from a family on the other side of the bay. Out of the plastic bag, a charred pig's head is poking out, and two cloven hooves. The present is scraped clean of meat, which is served as dinner.

And somebody has begun to drink alcohol and become noisy.

A kind daddy is carrying around his three small children and feeds the biggest one, who is ill.

The pastor's wife is in hospital with severe malaria. The week before they had to take her in a motorboat to the hospital in Atoifi, in pouring rain and rough seas. It took 1½ hours. The pastor will visit her tomorrow. But he cannot afford any petrol for the boat ride. Happily, he tells me that he has found a shortcut on land, but only at low tide. So now, he will paddle for half an hour and then walk for another hour. 'A shortcut...'

Midday...the sun is frying...I stretch out for a while...outside I hear voices in Kwaio...the language I associate with affiliation and protection...the waves are gurgling at the shore...my eyelids are heavy... Zzzz...

In the afternoon, Grandfather Jimmy has formed a little brigade. They are chopping and clearing a part of the jungle to make a football field, but it is boggy in the middle.

A woman has bought a bale of second-hand clothes in Honiara. The clothes are imported from Australia, and now she is trying to sell them in Gounabusu. We are trying on clothes and giggling. Before, I had felt some distance towards me from some women, but suddenly everything is totally familiar: women, shopping, clothes. Many try, but few buy; $5-10 for skirts and blouses is too expensive, not to mention a pair of jeans for $25. Nobody has any cash, and the woman has had to lower the prices and doesn't even know if she can cover her own purchasing costs.

This could be paradise, if it were not for the fact that this is an ordinary village with ordinary people. Everybody is, in other words, individuals with different personalities, wishes and needs. And maybe that's the way it is: Paradise is inside ourselves.

Food and meals

The bulk of Solomon Islands' cooking, and by all means in the whole Pacific, is kumara, sweet potato. In Fousisigi it is cultivated high up on the mountainsides. It is dug up by the women with a stick, washed and stored in the kitchen. When it is to be cooked, the women peel and boil it. The skin is boiled separately and given to the pigs. The peeling is usually done with a bush knife or small knife. But now, a small widget has appeared in the stores; a peeler for $3.50. I had brought a number of them, and they became appreciated presents. The peeling became as easy as one, two, three.

As mentioned, in the villages they cook without any exception on an open fire in a separate kitchen. It is also the most common way in the towns, although kerosene and gas are used by some. Electric or gas stoves inside the houses are very unusual.

Kumara is usually served with kabis: slippery kabis or any other vegetables. This is washed, cleaned, chopped and boiled in coconut milk or fried in oil (if you can afford oil, have access to a store or have a relative who has brought oil).

You get coconut milk by grating the fruit meat from ripe, brown coconuts on a scraper, mixing it with water and squeezing it with your hands. It produces a thick white liquid, resembling milk. (Coconut water, on the other hand, is what you drink directly from unripe green coconuts. This liquid is transparent, resembling water.) I tell the villagers that there are no coconuts growing in Sweden. They are sometimes imported, but they are small and usually rancid. There is also tinned coconut milk, which is expensive. The villagers feel sorry for people in Sweden. I have also showed photos from my kitchen in Sweden and again, they feel sorry for the Swedes who must *stand up* when cooking!

To that kabis mix you may, depending on economy and access, add noodles and/or tayio. If somebody has no kabis, noodles or tayio, then only 'dry' kumara is served. ('Dry' means without anything else added. 'Dry tea' means coffee without any cakes.) If they are lucky in the village, they may occasionally catch fish. You may assume that fish could be caught in abundance at any time, but fish is dependent on seasons and is not always available. Some fish are small, under 10 cm, and full of bones.

Small children, both at the coast and in the mountains, have a tendency for swollen stomachs, which could be a sign of lack of protein.

As an alternative to kumara there are the other root crops: cassava, taro, idu, pana, yam. All of them are filling and rich with starch, leaving a stubborn film in pots and on the teeth. Rice is city food and a luxury. Traditionally, there are no spices in local cooking. However, in town, you can buy curry or soy sauce to give a little zest to the meal.

Kumara is, as previously mentioned, the basic food and can be monotonous, even if there are innumerable possibilities of preparing:

– boiled peeled kumara
– boiled unpeeled kumara
– fried kumara
– motu-baked kumara
– soup of kumara in coconut milk

And kumara can be served with vegetables, or with tayio or, at Christmas, with pork, also in all shapes (boiled, fried, etc.)

Taro is a powerful crop. It may be boiled, but the very best way of cooking is placing it in the embers of a cooking fire. After some time, you scrape the charred surface and eat the content, which has become soft.

One feast dish is 'pudding', which consists of mashed root crops (cassava or taro) with or without banana, baked in a motu. One kind of pudding is *hongi*.

Do you want to make hongi? Grate uncooked taro. Take *karisi* leaves or banana leaves and pull them quickly over fire to scorch them. Lay them in a suitable tray and rub them with coconut milk. Cover the leaves with half of the mashed taro and press it flat. Add more coconut milk, then a new layer of taro and finish with coconut milk. Make a parcel of the leaves and cover the pudding. Bake in a motu around one hour.

It is difficult to define traditional meals. Sometimes, three meals are served: breakfast at 7-8 a.m., lunch at 1-2 p.m. and dinner after sunset. There is no special food for breakfast; usually the leftovers from the evening before, and for lunch, something simple. The evening dinner is the main meal. Sometimes, especially on Sundays, the breakfast and lunch are replaced with a 'brunch' at 10-11 a.m. Many families say grace before you are allowed to begin eating. Otherwise, there are no ceremonies such as a 'toast', etc. Nor is there any rule that everyone must be gathered, or that everyone must be served, before you can dig in. Melanesia is refreshingly free from formalities and ceremonies!

It is common to give an extra portion to a nearby household. Also, if some of them have guests, they too get a serving, especially the children of the guests. Everybody is expected to follow these rules, so it will balance out in the end. It is good practise to share, and gifts are returned. If there is not enough food, the children will eat first. At big feasts with a buffet table, the children will again eat first, then the women and finally the men.

After the food, you drink water, usually directly from a bottle which is passed around. You drink without touching the bottle neck with the lips, for the sake of hygiene. The most honourable person drinks first, and the bottle must then be full.

Robert and I would go 'home' to Fousisigi many times during the following years. Being city folks, we are spoilt with a varied menu. For our visits we bring some 'city goods' and share with the villagers. So sometimes, for breakfast we offer bread or biscuits, marmalade or peanut butter. But these are modernities and not very healthy. We try otherwise to eat local food as much as possible. In the evenings, we give Coffeemix. The elderly especially, who feel the cold, enjoy a warm cup of coffee with lots of sugar.

Photo 21

To the gardens
The path is steep. I am puffing and sloshing in mud, armed with water, sunhat, a dig-stick and an empty sack. All the time, I must look at the ground, so as not to stumble on stones and roots. My flip-flops are twisting and turning. Either you should be barefoot or wear trekking shoes. The others have no trekking shoes. When I raise my head, I can admire the extraordinary view over Sinaragu. The bay is fringed with green, green mountains, and in the middle of its mouth there is a tiny islet. I would like to have a longer look, try to take in where I am. But then I must make a stop, and then I will be behind the others.

I had joined some women and a ten-year-old boy to go up to their gardens in the mountains to get kumara. I considered it as a part of my visit, even if the women tried to dissuade me. Such attempts usually have the opposite effect, and so they had this time, too. But the way up *was* tiring.

After half an hour's walk, we were there. After a little rest, we poked with the dig-stick around the kumara mounds until we found the red-purple or pale-yellow tubers. We threw them down in a heap but not too far. If they rolled down the whole mountainside, they would be lost. And then we started weeding, and I began to feel very tired. The sun was hot, but here high up, a slight breeze was blowing, and that made it bearable. The women were mollycoddling me and told me to rest in the shade, but I tried to put an effortless look on my face: 'shame on him that gives in'.

When the women decided that we had enough, the kumara was packed in the sacks, a front-band was laid round our foreheads to carry a sack, and so we set off downwards. I thought that my neck might break in this way. It was almost inhumanly heavy, even if I had the lightest sack, only 12 kg, and now there was no longer a slight breeze.

'If you can't carry it, then Andrew can take over,' they said.

Andrew was the ten-year-old boy. Giving him my sack would be deeply humiliating for me and out of the question. I had only one thought in my head: *Let us be down, let us be down.* And now came the reward. The villagers' delight over my participation was touching but sad. They never thought 'Whites' could do 'such' things. Myself, I said that it was 'nothing'. If only they knew...

Later, I joined them in their gardens a few more times and hated it. The women do this every day, except Sundays. They are as strong as bears.

Handicraft

It was easier to participate in the art of making rain shields, sleeping mats, sun fans, baskets, plates and brooms by hand using pandanus or coconut leaves. Art is not quite the correct word, since these are articles for daily living, not for art. In the village, only some of the older women have mastered this handicraft. In Sweden I have been working with birch bark craft, and I definitely have it in my fingers.

Rain shields are made, usually by women, of pandanus leaves. Pandanus is called *mode* in Kwaio, and mode is also the name of the product, i.e., the rain shield or 'umbrella'. Leaves of 10-20 cm width are cut, trimmed and dried in the sun. The previously green leaves are now a beautiful gleaming yellow. They are hammered and pressed until they are smooth, woven in an intricate system, and then sewn together. In past years, the women used hibiscus fibres as a thread but nowadays the plastic strips from rice sacks. When the rain shields are new, they are totally rainproof. They are used until they mould or rot, and then the women just make new ones.

Sleeping mats and sun fans are made of 1-2 cm wide strips cut from pandanus leaves. They are woven cross-wise in the same way as birch bark or chippings in Sweden. The beautiful kastom baskets, which are the pride of East Kwaio, are all made with strips of only a few millimetres, and here enters the artistic aspect: the women strive to make a beautiful pattern.

The women also make brooms of coconut leaves, using the long, thin leaflets on both sides of the leaf stem. The green is removed, and the naked leaflet stem is trimmed. Once you have enough leaflet stems for a broom, you join them, either by weaving the soft ends or, to make it easy, simply bundle them with a rubber band.

Baskets, plates, sun fans, trays and other smaller things are made of coconut leaflets. Sometimes the leaflet stem is kept, to make the product stronger.

I made a basket of coconut leaflets, following the technique of birch bark weaving. The villagers were very interested and asked about the material. I explained it as *bark blong special tree*. Now the basket is standing there as a monument of Swedish-Solomon cultural exchange. One woman wanted to put laundry pegs in it, which is a perfect use. But coconut leaflets are not as sturdy and strong as birch bark.

Photo 22

Canoe sealing

Old Uncle Sale looked worried as he rubbed his face, which showed signs of a previous stroke. He had problems. His canoe was leaking and taking in water. Bailing was not enough anymore; it had to be sealed. He cut a square hole in the canoe, the size of a hand, and, from a piece of wood, he cut a corresponding square. He pressed the piece into the hole and pounded it with a hammer. However, the wood piece had to be sealed.

The day before I had found some fruits from the *muki* tree. The fruit looks like a small brown avocado or a big smooth brown kiwi. Robert told me that they were used for canoe sealing, and I picked them up. Now, I gave them to Uncle Sale, proud to know the use of the natural material. He was indeed very happy, and together we crushed the pink fruit meat and created a natural sealant.

But Uncle Sale was not satisfied (and then it was not so cute and ecologically friendly anymore). He looked around; something was missing. He shouted an order in Kwaio to a young girl. She searched and then brought a torch battery, A-size. He crushed it and mixed the black-dotty content with the pink muki meat. Then he put it on the splices of the canoe and left it all to dry. The sealant was no longer the beautiful natural and organic seal.

The hidden people

The hidden people have been mentioned here and there in this book. They live their traditional life in the mountains of East Kwaio. Nowhere and never has the kastom concept been stronger than here. The hidden people have rejected Christianity and until just recently also clothes and other modern inventions. They live a traditional lifestyle with shifting cultivation and move from place to place to be close to their gardens.

A typical village is built on a hillside, with the men's house situated highest. That is where the men gather for discussing important things and for contact with the ancestral spirits, and usually where the men's taboo place is located: the skull house. Below the men's house are the common dwellings, where men, women and children live in nuclear families. Lower down are the menstruation house and the childbirth house, where the women stay when needed: the women's taboo place. Even farther down are the toilet places, but there are no buildings for that; it is performed straight in the bush.

All houses are built of easily accessible material like bamboo and sago palm. The villagers make most of their tools and weapons (spears, bows and arrows) themselves but buy knives and axes from the coastal markets or from town.

The religion is based on ancestral spirits, andalo, and the contact between the spirits and the common people is mediated through the priest. The ancestral spirits are constantly present and rule the lives of the people. They must not be offended or insulted, such as when somebody breaches a taboo. A breaching demands purification and sacrifice to the spirits. The most common way is the sacrifice of special pigs, who are slaughtered and eaten by the priest and other men. These pigs are special insofar that they are named after a certain ancestor. Some even assert that they *are* the ancestors, in a different dimension. Only men who are descendants from this ancestor are allowed to eat their meat. In addition, there are ordinary pigs 'without name' which may be eaten by anyone.

Food eaten by men and boys is cooked and served separately from the food eaten by women and girls. Also plates, cups and containers for water, i.e., hollow bamboo canes, are separate.

The culture or kastom of the Kwaio in general, and the hidden people in particular, is founded on the concept of opposites like 'purity – pollution' and 'high – low'. The view of purity has an almost ritual quality, and to avoid pollution, there are, as we have seen, several restrictions and rules. The difference is that for the Christian Kwaio it is a recommendation, while for the hidden people it is an absolute law.

The relations between the hidden people and their Christian relatives are sometimes tense. If somebody from the hidden people visits a Christian family, the latter might pray intensely afterwards, to 'cast out the devil'. The missionaries have told them that the hidden people worship the devil. But the concept 'devil' was introduced by the Christian missionaries and has no place in the traditional Kwaio religion.

One may believe that the hidden people have always lived isolated until now. But they used to have, and still have, active contacts with the rest of the country and the world. During the 19th century, it was common for young men to seek their fortunes with a few years of work in other islands or even in other countries. Most of them returned to their village, strong in their culture but with broader perspectives. Others settled overseas. For example, a colony was formed in Fiji, which is still active today. Some young men recently visited their ancestors' land in Solomon Islands. They have lost their language, but not their roots.

Nowadays, many of the hidden people move permanently to the Christian coastal villages. Many elders have followed their children; who would take care of them otherwise? They have apparent difficulties in adapting and will not step foot inside the church. Sitting in the doors of their houses, they look at life in the coastal village with scepticism. The women are tough and smoke pipes. The hidden people are on the whole more reserved than their coastal wantoks. They have a dignity about them and are definitely not inclined to laughter and goofing off. The children are quiet, do not lark around or horseplay like their coastal cousins. But they soon learn.

Why this ongoing stream of hidden people moving to the coast? Attracted by the easier life? The possibility of employment which gives cash? Attracted by the individualistic images of Solomon Christianity, in contrast to the collective social order in the mountains? Many priests are authoritarian; they are the ones who have contact with the ancestral spirits. (Not to say that Christian priests may not be authoritarian, too!) Concerns about the rules for the women? A desire to be like everybody else? The questions build up.

Photo 23

Gender roles and femininity

Most of the daily duties are indisputably done by the women. They care for the gardens in the mountains and perform most of the household work. Although they have a strenuous life, they don't rush or stress, and there is always time for chatting and singing and a moment to nap. The men go fishing, slaughter and butcher pigs. Of course, the last-mentioned does not happen every day. It is also the men's work to grate and mash kumara and cassava for pudding, which is quite heavy work. Both sexes may cook, wash clothes and chop firewood, but it is primarily done by women. For big feasts, everybody prepares the food together. Otherwise, traditional men don't do very much except carry around the small children or 'sit under a tree and talk about "important things", waiting for dinner' (said by Robert).

The women's primary duty is to keep the house neat and in good order. The men's primary duty is to defend the house and the family. That was of course very important once, during times of warfare. Nowadays, there is not much to defend oneself from.

In the traditional Melanesian society there were, and are, strict rules and restrictions around femininity and fertility. Generally speaking, there are more restrictions for women than for men. Traditions and customs vary between the countries (e.g., Vanuatu and Solomon Islands) and between provinces within the same country (e.g., Makira and Isabel) or between ethnic groups within the same province (e.g., Kwaio and Kwara'ae), and between rural and urban, but there is a common core. Kwaio is said to be the strictest group of all.

The traditional Melanesian restrictions, taboos, for women are:

– not stand higher than a man;
– not sit on or step over food, e.g., rice sacks, or food utensils, e.g., pots;
– not carry food under something (e.g., a house built on posts);
– not step over a fireplace;
– not sit on a monument with a name;
– not step over a stream with water for drinking or cooking;
– not climb a staircase if somebody is sitting underneath;
– not hang skirts or underwear to dry too visibly;
– not show anything between the waist and the knees;
– not touch a man outside the family, or a man's bag (however, shaking hands in a formal situation is acceptable);
– not visit a male taboo place, i.e., the skull house.

Men, on the other hand, are expected to:

– not stand lower than a woman;
– not go under anything, e.g., a clothing line, or (in town) an underpass;
– not visit a female taboo place, e.g., a menstruation house.

Both sexes are told to:

– not pass too close in front of somebody;
– not pass between two persons in communication;
– not step over somebody's outstretched legs or body;
– not give somebody a present if others see it;
– not show emotions in public. (Many couples of the same sex are seen holding hands. This is not a sign of homosexuality but of friendship.)

Homosexuality is formally illegal, but the general attitudes are quite tolerant.

How important is it for a foreigner to follow these rules? The rules are relaxed in town but stricter in villages and before the elderly. Some rules are less important than others. If a foreigner follows a rule that is less important, it will lead to appreciation. But if she or he breaches a rule that is more important, it may cause offense. Therefore, the safest course would be to follow them all. And people will hardly say anything *to* you, but surely *about* you!

Restrictions surrounding a woman's body are, or were, especially important, particularly dealing with menstruation. During menstruation, the woman is not allowed to/does not need to (depending on the perspective one adopts) stay with the others. Instead, she stays in a secluded taboo area. This area differs between the various Melanesian ethnic groups.

Among the Langa Langa in Malaita this restriction is not followed anymore. But in the old time, she used to stay in a special women's area where she cooked for herself and the youngest children. Other women could come and visit her and bring her food. The boys were allowed to stay there until they were around seven or eight years old. But, as a Langa Langa man told me with a glint in his eye, if an older boy had done some mischief and his daddy was chasing him, the boy could slip into the women's area, to which the adult men had no access.

Among the Kwaio there were, and are, stricter rules. In some groups, only the menstruating women were allowed to stay in the area – no other women, no children. If a woman was breastfeeding, others brought the baby for the feeding, but then the baby was taken back and nursed by others. The woman did not receive food or anything else from outside. Everything was cultivated within the area. If her cooking fire had died, she was allowed to get fire from outside, but only if the piece of wood had been lighted indirectly, from the others' 'pure' households via a third piece of wood, which was then thrown away. Nowadays, the practise of menstruation houses only exists among the hidden people.

Who benefits from this system? One may discuss it from a gender perspective. The most common explanation is that the woman is polluted and in possession of dangerous powers during her menstruation, which the rest of the community, especially the men, must protect themselves from. But the women themselves benefit from this system. Many women are more receptive to infections during these days; they feel pain and are in general more fatigued. This gives her a period of rest. In the menstruation house she can stay in peace and not attend to others. In discussing the question of Kwaio's menstruation houses, Roger Keesing stated that a practise stays alive only as long as the individuals support it.

Menstruation hygiene articles? In olden times and among the hidden people, women use leaves and moss. Women of the coastal villages use rags. The women living in towns purchase pads and tampons from the stores.

Restrictions likewise surround childbirth. The woman does not deliver indoors, but outdoors, called 'bush delivery'. If it is her first baby, she may be accompanied by some older women; if not, she is alone. After the delivery, the woman spends some time in a special childbirth hut which she has built in advance. The length of the time varies between the different Melanesian ethnic groups, from ten days up to one month. Other women bring food, and the new mother can rest and devote all her time to the baby. After this isolation, different rituals of purification follow. Among the hidden people, the women shave their own head and the baby's down. In the olden times, they used sharpened bamboo sticks, nowadays Bic razors. After this ritual, mother and child are accepted into the community.

Some women, who go into the bush when the labour pains begin, never return. Sometimes skeletons are found, one large and one small, and at times nothing at all.

Currently, most women deliver in hospitals, as long as they can afford a taxi or petrol for a motorboat. If the baby comes too fast, there will be a *bush delivery* or *sanbis delivery*, the latter a delivery on the beach. However, a delivery must never, ever take place in the dwelling house. It would be considered polluted for eternity.

Another taboo relates to urination. A woman is not allowed under any circumstances to pee inside the dwelling house, in a chamber pot or such. Otherwise the family has to tear down the house and build a new one. And/or sacrifice a pig.

And again, these taboos are more or less abandoned and are practised solely among traditional Kwaio and/or the hidden people.

Clothes

One area where the rules actually are getting stricter at the transition to a 'modern' lifestyle is clothes. According to tradition, among the hidden people they wear no, or hardly any, clothes at all. Only married women wear a small blue apron, which just covers their genitalia. Nowadays, following the arrival of Christianity into the Kwaio culture, most islanders wear 'European' clothes, such as t-shirts, blouses, shorts and knee-length skirts. Hardly any headdress except baseball caps for some men.

Clothes are sold in abundance in the towns, either new ones or second-hand. New ones largely imported from China cost $30-60 which is considered expensive. Second-hand clothes vary in price, from some that are much higher than the new ones to $5 for 'a full plastic bag'. Second-hand clothes are a big and flourishing business in town.

And as mentioned, the hidden people are beginning to wear clothes to a much greater extent. Before, they put on clothes only when they went down the muddy mountain paths to the coast. Either to visit relatives or, at the Friday market, exchange betel nuts and tobacco for knives, razors and matches. When they returned home, they took off their clothes again. Nowadays, they keep them on. Why, I wonder.

Clothes have many purposes. The primary one is maybe protection from cold. But that is hardly applicable here, at least in daytime. Another purpose is to cover the naked body, which may be seen as shameful. But that perspective doesn't exist among the hidden people. Yet another purpose is to mark status and power. But the Kwaio have hardly any pronounced leaders, and those who lead are known anyway. To be like everybody else? But the Kwaio have always been proud in keeping their own lifestyle intact. Apart from this, clothes cost money, which the hidden people usually lack. And the Kwaio have always done well without clothes before. So why now? I have no answer to that question.

Floating families

Generally speaking, people circulate; they float around between the islands, live for a few months here, a few months there, with relatives, for work or for social intercourse. I found the same phenomenon in Vanuatu. Living together seems to be less couple-oriented than in Sweden. It is not necessarily the spouse who is the most important adult in a person's life. Siblings, cousins, and friends are just as important, if not even more so.

Even the children float around, which is the part I find the most difficult to understand (not saying that I think it is strange, wrong or abnormal). As soon as the children have been weaned and have learnt to eat by themselves, they can start floating around, living a month or six months at a time with various relatives on different islands. A family with, say, eight children can have two children living elsewhere but, at the same time, have two other children staying with them. The Swedish writer and anthropologist Bengt Danielsson made the same observations in French Polynesia.

Following this pattern, a family close to me with small children left their firstborn, a two-year-old boy, with his paternal grandmother on a completely different island for half a year. The explanations were somewhat vague: By doing this the parents would be able to be more engaged in their farming, in the one-year-old baby sister, etc. One explanation was: 'It's *possible*; he's big enough now to eat by himself'. They probably found my 'Why?' a bit strange and I am very careful not to explicitly compare with Sweden. If they think it is OK, then... No one seemed to fare badly; the boy lived happily, knowing that he was loved and welcome everywhere. But in this way the parents missed out on their firstborn's explosive language and motor development, and didn't they *long for* their little one? (His mother later told me that she did weep when the ship sailed off.)

Along with the little boy came a cousin as his nursemaid, a six-year-old girl who, because of this, was separated from *her* family. The girl's nine-year-old brother lived with his paternal grandfather on a third island, etc. (Those grandparents were not divorced or anything like that.)

So, when I left for Sweden for a short visit a woman asked me,

'Can't you please bring a little Swedish baby back with you? It would be so nice to cuddle with it.'

I gave some sort of vague answer to the effect that I didn't think any parent would want to let them go so far away. The climate is too hot, etc.

Yet the people here in Melanesia could just as well ask the opposite question:

'Why do parents in Sweden keep their children with them for so long?'

That's the question.

Child rearing

The two youngest toddlers in the family (two and three years old or, to be exact, born within nine months of each other) are wild. They are yelling and screaming and out of control, throwing food around and chasing each other during meals. The two-year-old girl has attacks of rage around five o'clock every afternoon. Nobody cares.

Everyone cuddles babies. When their mothers have breastfed them, they can park them in the arms of more or less anyone over five years old and thereby get time to do other things. I think of Sweden, where it is often *one* person, usually the mother, or at most *two*, who take care of a baby. Here, it is a whole village. What it means for consensus and harmony I do not need to explain.

Small children are generally reared gently and without violence. However, 'reared' is maybe not the correct word. They are allowed to do whatever they wish; nobody chides or punishes them. On the other hand, nobody reacts when they are screaming and crying. Nobody comforts them or picks them up. They are simply ignored until they stop screaming, which they do soon. Then they are carried around unlimitedly. Children are considered everyone's children, and there are always arms to rest in. They are carried around, and they sit on everyone's laps, old or young, woman or man. They never lack attention or physical contact.

The children sleep wherever they happen to be located when they feel tired. Well, indoors, of course, and with persons they know. For the parents, this is excellent – they get a night by themselves.

At the age of six or seven, in most cases, there is a dramatic change in the children's lives. Now they meet responsibilities as family members. They are expected to accept their duties in the house: carry water, chop firewood, grate coconuts, look after their small siblings. Of course, adapted to their ability. Girls must help more in the household than boys. A seven-year-old girl will do the duties of an adult woman without complaining: wash, sweep and carry the small siblings. But there is always time for play.

The children begin school. And they fulfil the new demands. Previously self-centred and wild, they are now helpful, friendly and harmonic.

In some families, there are no expectations of more mature behaviour, even when the children are bigger. For example, I have seen twelve-year-olds push smaller children, even beat them, without any reprimand from the adults. In other families, this would lead to physical punishment.

But somehow, the children slide smoothly into the role of adults, from totally wild toddlers to responsible family members, sort of by themselves. Gangs of 'toughies' do exist in town, but there are not many.

There is domestic violence in many families. The authorities carry on campaigns against this. On the radio, they warn against using violence and hard words towards the children, 'because then they will turn it against the parents, when they grow bigger'. So true.

Conflict

Once, after dinner, there was a sudden rampant weeping in the living room. I rushed in, appalled. It was Aunty Kwaleka, wailing loudly. Her thin body shook as she cried. The other family members whispered that one of the teenage girls had been snooty to her. She cried louder and louder. It almost sounded as if she were doing it on purpose. I resisted the impulse to go and comfort her; I was a stranger, an outsider. But why weren't the others doing anything? In my eyes, this was incomprehensible. Kwaleka was the oldest family member; where was their respect for the elderly? Nobody comforted her, nobody even rebuked the girl who apparently caused it. They muttered that Kwaleka was old, that the girl should have known better and so on, but nobody spoke directly to the girl. Everybody waited until the old woman stopped crying. Then they all went about their business.

If respect for elders is a Melanesian virtue, why hadn't the others done anything? Are they *so* afraid of conflict? If self-control is a Melanesian virtue, why had Aunty Kwaleka cried so openly and so loudly that it almost sounded not real? The questions built up.

On another occasion, a 15-year-old girl was beaten by a peer because she happened to fart while she was asleep. Doubly humiliated, she too cried profusely while everybody stood in a ring watching her cry. Nobody did anything.

On yet another occasion, a ten-year-old boy was pushed off a chair by his older brother. Nobody said anything.

Several times I experienced the same thing: a conflict with an obvious victim and an obvious perpetrator, but nobody stepping in.

Folk belief

The fireflies are twinkling like little flying torches. They mostly appear just after dusk. If they appear around midnight, they are not fireflies but evil ancestral spirits. If such an evil spirit enters your house, it means that a family member is going to die. You can prevent this by saying,

'You frighten me; leave my house' but *not by killing it*. (Think of the Swedish reluctance to kill a spider...)

Ancestral spirit, evil spirit, ghost, devil: all have the same name in Kwaio: 'andalo'. The bigger boys frightened two-year-old Small Tome with andalo:

'Be careful, andalo is coming to take you, boohoohoo'. They spread their fingers and distorted their voices. The two-year-old cried out in fear at night and saw andalo everywhere. When he saw my wooden Nguzunguzu-head he said 'andalo'. Nguzunguzu is not a part of the Kwaio culture, and Small Tome had never seen any image like that before; still, he immediately knew to say 'andalo'.

Other phenomena bordering folk belief are healing and sorcery. They all go hand in hand with religion. Those with the deepest belief in these folk traditions may also be the most frequent churchgoers.

An academic family

Nobody can know Malaita without a visit to Auki. The town seems deceptively small and sleepy, with one main (short) street, two parallel streets and two cross-streets. But once you have gone around the settlements up towards the mountains, you realize how big the town actually is, and how dynamic. Auki is the new centre after Honiara. The new harbour extension and the new market building are signs of this. From Honiara, you arrive in three hours with a speed boat or in six hours with a cargo-passenger ship.

In Auki lived, and live, my old tour-guide Ronnie and his wife Elsie, an academic couple. They have four children, of which three are teen-agers and one a four-year-old, and they live with a number of more or less temporary relatives. Ronnie, an environmental consultant, is doing further education in Honiara (and in 2020, he is in politics!), and Elsie is a primary school teacher.

While staying in Fousisigi, I had some shopping to do in Auki, so I took a motorboat and a truck to get there. I visited Ronnie and Elsie, and they asked me to stay with them for some time, which I gratefully accepted. We enjoy each other's company, and it was a welcome change from the village.

The family did, and does, not live in a palm leaf house like Robert and me but in a permanent house, painted a cheerful blue. The house has a living room and three bedrooms. Two wooden sofas, two small tables, a chest of drawers, a bookshelf and a bed are the only furniture in the whole house. The parents sleep in the bed, daughters and female relatives on mattresses on the floor. Sons and male relatives sleep in the kitchen. Cooking is done over an open fire. Firewood is collected from the jungle on the other side of the road.

At the time for my visit, the big problem was *water*: for cooking, dishwashing, laundry and personal hygiene for, say, 10 persons. The house was designed for plumbing and there was a sink, but unfortunately, the house was not yet connected to the town water supply. Instead, the family had to rely on a rainwater tank and two discarded fridges, laid on their 'backs' to collect rainwater. During the dry season the lack of water might become quite concerning. Occasionally, the family must go to a river 10 km away to dishwash, and on Sundays ever farther to another river to wash clothes. The family owned a taxi with an employed driver, and he was the one who was driving us. In order to simplify the book-keeping, they paid full price to him (and got it back later). Take a taxi for dishwashing. My, my. The children were joining us, swimming, splashing and diving from the bridge.

Ronnie and Elsie had neither water nor electricity, but they had, like us, invested in a solar panel on the roof. Theirs was bigger and more expensive (c. $18,000, a half year's salary for a teacher). It produced enough power to run a fan *or* a few hours of TV *or* radio. So they have to choose.

In a palm leaf hut with a tin roof, a toilet bowl stood as a throne. For flushing, you must haul up water from a well outdoors and pour it inside the bowl.

The school term had started, and the mornings were very busy; everybody was going to work, school and preschool. The fire must be lit, water boiled and the two pigs fed. Our breakfast consisted of buns, which a neighbouring woman was baking and selling, and Coffeemix.

Then I was alone in the house. I washed the breakfast dishes in a sink beside the 'lying' fridge – it had been raining during the night, so there was plenty of water – swept the house, the stairs and the kitchen, shooed away the three dogs and some hens. I carried away peels and other vegetable waste to the compost under the banana plants. The family made jokes about me being their house girl. It was very pleasant to stay with this family in their everyday life.

It was also touching and enlightening to see how these resilient, patient people were working hard to make life go on. These were well-educated persons with relatively well-paid jobs as compared to the farmers in Fousisigi with their subsistence economy. It is difficult to say which ones were living the hardest life. In the village, they had no employment to stress them, and they had free food. This academic family was inside the monetised economy and must pay for everything. And most things were expensive.

Personal hygiene was working, too. *Given that there was limited water.* I thought about what a good life I had in Honiara, certainly in a leaf house but with unlimited running water. Water means *everything*.

Elsie was, and is, as previously mentioned, a teacher. One day I joined her at her work. She had 45 pupils in her classroom. Half of them had desks; others were sitting on the floor. The schoolbooks for the little six- to seven-year-old children were in English, and she explained in Pijin. The pedagogy was exemplary. With enthusiasm, encouragement and simple means she raised the ability of every pupil. The worn-down classroom was filled with homemade pedagogic pictures and the pupils' own works. Her own little girl had been picked up from preschool, 'kindy'. She was drawing while her mother was teaching, but she had difficulty staying quiet.

After Elsie had written a report of the school day, we went together to the market for shopping: rice, coconuts, kabis, kumara, fish. At home, we relaxed, weeded in the garden. The teenagers met their friends or sang in the church choir.

In the evening, we cooked in the kitchen and ate in the dwelling house. Chatting on the cool veranda. The little girl was singing in a shrill voice:

'I am so happy, I am so happy, as happy as can be, I am so happy, I am so happy, because Jesus loves me.'

After this, there was time for homework. Everybody gathered under the only bulb, sitting or lying on the floor. Elsie put the little girl to sleep and prepared the lessons for the next day. The dishwashing would be done early tomorrow morning by Julia, a girl around 18 years old.

We were sitting in the living room. Some were talking, playing guitar or listening to the radio, which would be the only power-consumer of the day. A carpenter with a Rasta hairdo had built a gate to keep out the dogs from the veranda. A by-passing man was selling fish from his bicycle. The pigs were grunting, the hens were clucking, the dogs were sleeping (but they would make a hell of a noise at night). The evening cool surrounds the house.

Shell money

Malaita also includes the beautiful Langa Langa Lagoon, with its artificial islands. While I already was on the west coast of Malaita, I might as well go there and see the making of shell money. Ronnie took me there. He said we would go at eight o'clock; he woke up at nine and said we were going at ten... 'Solomon time', it's called. And around eleven we took off southwards along Malaita's west coast through profuse greenery to the lagoon.

The lagoon stretches along a large part of Malaita's west coast. Here, the villagers have attached stones and dead corals to the shallow sea bottom. In this way, they have built artificial islands. On these islands, there are traditional dwelling houses, kitchens, pig pens and chicken pens, and bushes and coconut palms grow. But there is no soil for agriculture, so people paddle in canoes to their gardens on the mainland. They drink water from rainwater tanks. Or coconuts. The people here speak their own language: Langa Langa.

Langa Langa and Kwaio are the main two regions in Solomon Islands with active making of shell money even today, but the Langa Langa style is the most wide-spread one. This shell money is famous all over Solomon Islands, yes, in the whole Pacific. In every corner of this lagoon, there are small family workshops, and at one family we could follow this process of shell money making. They wanted $20 for a demonstration, compared to another workshop which wanted $500 for the same thing.

The craft artists – usually women – begin with small pieces of white, black, brown or grey seashells, found on the beach or, for the rare red ones, dived for outside the reef. They chisel these pieces into tiny disks. The disks are drilled and threaded on a special strong wire and polished until they are round and smooth, just a few millimetres in diameter. The smaller, the more valuable. Then the disks are threaded on one-meter-long strings, which are tied in bundles, *tafule'au*, usually by ten. One string is worth $100 and a bundle of ten accordingly $1,000.

With these tiny disks, the craft artists can also make jewellery such as necklaces and headbands in intricate designs. At the market in Honiara in 2006, you could buy earrings for $5. (In 2020 they cost $30...) Shell money is used as means of payment. You cannot exactly pay the car mechanic with it, but it is used in traditional kastom transactions between families or villages. One example is compensation (financial penalty or 'fines') at different kinds of conflicts. Also, in case of a debt, shell money can be given as a pawn or deposit until the debt is paid.

But the most common use is the one of bride price. The parents of the boy give shell money to those of the girl. A common bride price is 50 bundles of ten, which means $50,000 to get married. The price of a new car, a staggering sum. If the boy and his parents had to pay this themselves, many men would stay unmarried. But the whole family and all the relatives make contributions; everybody has a plastic bag with shell money in some corner, for example from *their* daughter's marriage. All goes around. A small part of the shell money, especially that in the form of jewellery, belongs to the girl herself as a security, for example in case of divorce.

After this sojourn to the west coast of Malaita, I was happy to return to the east coast, to Fousisigi, rich of experience and knowledge. Truck and motorboat again...

Photos 24-26

Our 'holiday house'

Robert and I had spent almost two months in Fousisigi. With the exception of the little detour to Auki and Langa Langa Lagoon, we had been living a very quiet life, without mobiles, TV, radio, electricity. Robert been meeting countless relatives, and I increased my skills in traditional cooking and in the Kwaio language.

We were staying with Robert's brother, altogether 11 persons plus all the temporary guests. We had a room without windows, and it was beginning to feel a little crowded. Thus, the idea came up of building a house of our own. None of us wanted to stay in Fousisigi permanently, but a little 'holiday house' could be nice. In addition to that, we would have more privacy.

We chose a beautiful place in the little village with a view over Sinaragu, just opposite the little islet in the middle. Cousin Tome was consulted. It would not be a leaf house like the one we have in Honiara but a permanent wooden one. Tome was enthusiastic and immediately began planning. He had advanced training as a carpenter but never had the chance to build a whole house from the beginning to the end. Now he could finally get to use his knowledge!

The timber we got directly from the jungle. The forest and the land are owned by the village, thus by ourselves. During a few days, Robert and some men went up in the mountain with chainsaws, and soon the bay was buzzing with their sound. The timber was rolled down the hillsides and then pulled by canoes to the village. In that way, it was quite cheap for us. We only paid for the petrol for the chainsaws.

In the village on the selected spot, the men started digging holes for the posts. They were digging by hand, not even with spades but with coconut shells, and before we left the village, the house frame was built.

One living room, one bedroom, veranda! How nice it would be. Tome promised us that the next time we came, he would have built walls, windows and doors. We promised to buy paint in Honiara and send it with the next ship. Mild lime green it would be, we agreed.

Hmm, it turned out to be an aggressive neon green. I was about to cry, but the others in the village like it. They say it sort of brightens up the village. The whole bay, actually. Only a few can afford a wooden house, and nobody can afford paint. So now it stands there as the pride of the village, more elaborate than our house in Honiara. Later, the villagers built a little kitchen of green bamboo for us. Of course, it is not just a 'holiday house'. Since Robert counts Fousisigi as his real home, the house is a real dwelling house. When we are away, two unmarried men are staying inside.

Truck adventure

Like Christmas around the world, celebrating and meeting relatives could surely be a little overwhelming. It was, to put it mildly, person intense, and sometimes I felt somewhat isolated because of the language barrier. Sometimes I escaped indoors for 'sleep', although I just wanted to stay by myself, exhausted by social relations. (Sleeping is, as previously mentioned, an acceptable excuse to retire.) But needs like that come to me more and more seldom.

The youth, too, were complaining that they were bored. They were missing their friends in town.

So finally, it was time to go back. We decided not to await the cargo-passenger ship, which maybe would come next week, or next... Instead, we took the road via Auki.

Everybody was going back to Honiara, and *everybody* had mountains of baggage. The baggage now went the other way around and consisted of agricultural products like kumara and other root crops from their own gardens, homemade sit mats and baskets... And indeed, some more pigs...

And the road, the road. The road between Auki and Atori is the only one that goes across the island. It is not sealed, and after rains it is transformed into red puddles, becomes impassable and is closed. It didn't rain when we started. But then... The drops fell heavily and became harder and harder and more frequent. The truck stopped, we pulled a canvas over the tray, over passengers and baggage. The rain only increased.

Normally this route takes four hours. But now, the truck was so overloaded that a tyre exploded. The truck was careensing around, and an old man beside me almost fell from the tray. If I had not grabbed his arm, he would surely have fallen out onto the road. Every passenger and all the baggage had to be unloaded in the pouring rain. Since the truck could not move, and there was no mobile phone coverage, the driver had to go and try to borrow a car from a house. As luck would have it, the truck had chosen to have a flat tyre just outside an empty market place, and all the passengers went there en masse. We had started at four o'clock in the afternoon and gone halfway. It was still daylight when we reached the market, but it became dark fast. Many put things right; they made a fire and dried their soaked clothes. Robert and I ate a piece of *gwasu* (cassava pudding) we had brought, although I thought it smelled of rancid coconut. Then I tried to sleep, stretched out on a market bench of concrete, waiting, waiting and listening to the frogs. Frogs can be heard over several kilometres, and some species sound like woodpeckers.

Around ten in the evening, after four hours of waiting, came a *small* truck. The quickest passengers with the sharpest elbows climbed aboard. It was so crowded that they had to stand up and hold each other, but they were just happy to have a lift. We, the slow ones, were told that another truck was on its way. Cement and frogs again. It did, four hours later. Now it was two o'clock in the morning. I lay half asleep over a sack of kumara, tossed around, and feeling travelsick. I wanted to vomit. And just when the sun was rising over the horizon, we reached Auki.

Although the truck had stopped, I was still feeling sick, and from the tray I vomited onto the street. I suspect the rancid gwasu.

The voyage back home took three days, compared to the voyage out of a day and a half. This was on a Thursday, and the next ship to Honiara would not depart until Saturday. A relative to stay with was soon found. Then I had some kind of blackout, lying on a sleeping mat on the floor for one day and two nights, unable to get up. Sleeping and sleeping, body aching from the hard bedding.

On Saturday I managed to get up and board the *Tomoko*, kept sleeping on deck, and then, *poof*, we tumbled ashore and were at home in Honiara.

Time goes by

Back in town

I am back in Honiara, I am back in Honiara. After a sojourn in the home village it is always nice to come back to the bustling (well...) capital with its anonymity (well...), to meet all the friends again and enjoy all modern life. Exposure to goods! Electricity! Internet! TV shows: Solomon and Australian news and Miss Marple. With the help of radio, I am learning Pijin. Shopping at the market and in the innumerable Chinese stores. I realize what a city girl I am. Even though Fousisigi is 'home' for Robert, Honiara and Koa Hill are 'home' for me. *Lonely Planet Solomon Islands* (1977) hits the nail right on the head for me:

The Capital in Perspective

At first impression Honiara is a dusty, uneventful small town, with only a meagre selection of restaurants and some undistinguished shops. A couple of weeks in the provinces changes all that. After village life with no cars, no electricity, nowhere to eat out and (if you're lucky) a one-shelf store, the capital undergoes a magical transformation. It takes on the guise of a bustling and cosmopolitan metropolis, replete with culinary choices, shops heaving with consumer goods, and all the trappings of modern life, including traffic jams.

There were several internet cafés in town by then, 2009. It must have been one of the cheapest in the world ($20 for 1 hour). But ouch! I got a virus in my own laptop via my flash drive. A nice IT technician fixed it for $200 (a week's salary for unqualified work).

I check my email from Sweden and read mesmerized about something called a 'snowstorm'.

I am living an ordinary life. I have established routines for everything that was once new. Since Robert is driving, I have plenty of time to myself. Sometimes we meet in town and have lunch together, slipping into some kai-bar, or we buy fish and chips at the market and sit munching them at the harbour.

I hardly meet any other expatriates. Some are my friends: Anne-Maree from New Zealand who works in the Ministry of Fisheries & Marine Resources, Björn from Sweden/Australia at IFC/World Bank, Shanti from Malaysia/Australia and Sue from New Zealand/Australia, both in the Ministry of Culture & Tourism but in different departments. Actually, there are not so many more: the German consul, a pharmacist, the husband of a souvenir shop owner, then consultants, development workers, volunteers.

Natural catastrophes

The tragic natural catastrophes, the tsunami in Gizo in 2007 and the flooding in, Guadalcanal in 2009 have led to the setting up of the National Disaster Management Office. This organization is conducting intensive public information campaigns. Instructions on how to act if it happens again are printed in the telephone directory, and the radio repeats it frequently.

In 2009, several natural catastrophes occurred in south-east Asia and the Pacific, almost simultaneously (according to experts, in^-dependently of each other): earthquakes in Sumatra, Indonesia, and in the sea between Tonga, Samoa and American Samoa. The Philippines experienced a tornado with thousands of deaths. Some of my friends in Sweden contacted me, worried. A bit snootily, I replied that Solomon Islands is far away from these areas. Samoa is the same distance from Honiara as Bagdad is from London. And Sumatra is situated almost exactly between Solomon Islands and Sweden. So it might as well be *I* who was worried about *them*. Then I felt ashamed for my snootiness; of course, I was touched by their concern.

And I felt somewhat ill at ease about Samoa, considering that I had been there many times, had stayed in exactly the stricken area and had Samoan friends there. I had horrible direct reports from friends living there. I *could* have been there at just that time. Hmm! The reality was creeping closer!

But it would be closer than that, and now it was getting really unpleasant. One day, when I was sitting peacefully in an internet café, Robert called my mobile. His employer, RAMSI, had radar, and they had just discovered a rise in sea level after an earthquake in the ocean north of Vanuatu. There was a risk that this might cause a tsunami, and Vanuatu is very close to Solomon Islands. Robert told me to go to the Parliament building, which is located on a hill. Rumours began in the internet café.

Outside, in the street, this phone call seemed so unreal. Life went on as usual. Didn't people know anything? Should I warn them? Should I stand up and shout 'tsunami, tsunami'? I didn't. Here I was walking as a sleepwalker when I could save thousands of lives. I called Robert again and made objections:

'Here, nothing is happening. You are wrong.'

'They don't know anything, now go up to the Parliament!'

At the Parliament, some twenty persons had already gathered. Then more and more, and now it was beginning to feel real. Not only I had heard the warning; it was also broadcast on the radio. We sat silent or talking quietly, forming little groups seeking closeness to each other. It is remarkable how an outside danger can create bonds.

Some taxi drivers had parked their vehicles with their radios on, and after an hour and a half, we heard that the warning was cancelled. People began making their way down, but it was still a bit creepy. Along the main street, most stores were closed, but the market was open. I did my shopping in a hurry, while keeping an eye on the sea level, and then I went home. I am glad we are living some distance into the country and a little high. But our 'holiday house'! It is just a few flat metres from the shore.

The next day we learnt that no tsunami had ever developed in Vanuatu; the sea level had 'only' risen abnormally high.

Our own ethnic tensions

Right when I am having my shower at dusk, I can hear screaming and arguing. A gang of young boys is running past our house into the neighbouring area. There is the sound of fighting, with thuds and thumping. A pig is screaming desperately while being carried away. Then everything is quiet, very quiet. Around me, neighbours are talking in Kwaio and Pijin, shaken and upset – what are they saying, what are they saying? I am standing there in my wet lavalava and don't understand an iota. I can only hear fragments:

Kwara'ae...bad languis...Kwaio...kattem banana...stilim pikpik!

Little by little, the picture becomes clearer. A gang of young Kwara'ae boys have been swearing at some young Kwaio boys. This cannot go unpunished. Thus, the Kwaio gang attacks the neighbour, an adult man who has nothing to do with the row except being a Kwara'ae, cuts his banana stocks and steals his pig, which they slaughter and eat.

I feel ill at ease. There is a taste of Kristallnacht over it (the night in Germany 1938 when anti-Semites smashed the windows of the Jewish-owned shops). Persecution because of ethnic origin. And will Kwara'ae take revenge on Kwaio? Revenge tends to escalate. The next time maybe somebody's pig is not enough but instead somebody's...wife? Not exactly to slaughter and eat, but to harm in another way. A wife who is also a 'White' must be the ultimate revenge. It took several days before I dared to go out on my own, but eventually it seemed to have calmed down.

No wari 'Don't worry', said my family, and maybe there was no need to. I don't know how real my concerns were; maybe they were just loose imagination. But it shows how fragile the national identity is. Most Kwara'ae and Kwaio are friends. But Kwara'ae and Kwaio have a violent common history, and here is the combination of young men, and disillusionment, and alcohol, and aggression... The 'we-and-they phenomenon' can be seen all around the world.

House girls

When I am showing photos from Sweden, my relatives ask why I have no photo of my *haus gele*, 'house girl'. It is generally assumed that 'Whites' have house girls. Now, the Solomon Islanders want to copy. Here in town, in families where both spouses are working, it is common to employ a house girl.

These are new phenomena in Solomon Islands, both working families and employed house girls. There have always been young females who stay with their relatives and do household work for food and accommodation. But what is new is that it doesn't have to be relatives and the cash payment. The employers pay some hundred dollars a week for full-time work. But some girls are seriously exploited. A girl I know was working one *year* for a family and was paid $300!

'House girl' is an expression used by Solomon Islanders, while expatriates call them *haus mere*, 'house woman'. This is more appropriate, since many are adult women. Yet another, more neutral, designation is 'housekeeper'.

Vanuatu, a Duty-Free paradise?

It was in Vanuatu that my Melanesian odyssey began, a journey that would end with me settling down in Solomon Islands. After some years I returned, now with my Melanesian spouse and with Tore from Norway, my travel companion of many years.

We spent a few days in Port Vila and stayed at a cosy place, Tafea Guest House, with only local guests. Knowing Solomon Pijin, it was easy to communicate in Bislama. It was especially fun when I spoke to a vendor at the market. She immediately asked if I was from Solomon Islands.

'Oh yes,' I answered, delighted, 'but how do you know?'

'I can hear it when you speak,' she said. And then she had seen my Solomon kastom necklace. How exciting to have a Solomon identity! Otherwise, in Honiara I am usually classed as an Australian.

It was interesting to compare Vanuatu of today with the Vanuatu I remember from my first visit. There are both similarities and differences with Solomon Islands. The countryside is surely similar, but Port Vila is incredibly modern and fancy. Trendy shops in glass and concrete, coffee shops, restaurants, Duty Free-boutiques, real estate agencies. I did not see those things during my first visit. Has the city gone through some kind of metamorphosis, or do I remember wrongly? The streets are teeming with tourists. Around every second day during the season, there is a cruise ship anchoring in the harbour, and thousands of passengers stream out, mostly Australians. The prices skyrocket; the Australian dollar is the currency of the day. Tourism is a great source of income here, and different attractions are being presented, very professionally (and some of them overpriced): speed boats, deep sea fishing, helicopter tours, island nights. The beautiful bay is teeming with sailboats from all countries. Vanuatu has transformed into the South Pacific's Switzerland, or Dubai.

In Honiara, a cruise ship usually arrives every second month or so. Those tourists compare Port Vila and Honiara, and they say that *people are friendlier in Honiara*, and *the handicrafts are better*!

Before Independence in 1980, Vanuatu was controlled by both England and France, and the country still has three official languages: Bislama, English and French. The French influence in Port Vila is still strong. We were staying in a French *quartier* and bought *baguettes* in the *boulangerie* in the morning. Almost everything was much more expensive than in Honiara, but we cooked our own food and 'touristed' simply, to make it cheaper. For example, you can take the free ferry to the tiny island of Iririki with its luxurious hotel, stroll in their park, admire the sunset and maybe take a glass of orange in the bar. Not unexpectedly, Robert was the only dark-skinned guest there.

And we were going around by minibus. One difference between Solomon Islands and Vanuatu – which doesn't have to do with tourism – is the bus system. In Honiara, the buses only run along certain routes, and the passengers have to adapt their travel according to this. But in Port Vila, you tell the driver where you want to go, and then he combines an appropriate route, which suits all the passengers. A kind of collective taxi (and yes, they have ordinary taxis, too). Usually, you reach your goal quickly, but the bus could also be meandering through the whole of Port Vila. That will give you a free sightseeing tour.

Robert and I are mesmerized by this tax-free paradise of the South Pacific. Honiara seems like a backwater. Somehow, I feel bitter. Both countries have had more or less the same prerequisites, and Solomon Islands is definitely more 'laid back' (or 'an unpolished jewel' as one travel guide describes it). On the other hand, Port Vila is maybe losing its identity. The inhabitants are already selling off their land, the land, which is an inseparable part of Melanesian identity.

I don't want Honiara to become like Port Vila. It may sound like the fable 'The Fox and the Grapes' (where the moral is that you belittle what you cannot get), but I love my tousled Honiara. Some places in Honiara could possibly be smartened up. They could, for example, collect the rubbish or create a park on the empty ground between Mendana Avenue and the harbour or something (like the lovely seaside park in Port Vila). But not change too much.

Europe

Robert and I have travelled to Europe twice: 2008 and 2011. Robert, who had never been abroad, was eager to go, and even though I was less keen, I of course enjoyed showing him around.

So in 2008 we set off, going westwards by air via Brisbane, Kuala Lumpur and Copenhagen, and finally by train to Sweden. In Lund, my old home town, we stayed with my friends. We went to Stockholm, and from there we took a day cruise to Finland. And we visited our common friend Bob in Berlin. Finally, we ended our journey with one week in London and then took a flight back home via Los Angeles and Fiji. By this time we were both quite fed up with travelling, and instead of the planned one week in Fiji, we changed our stay there to just a sleep-over.

In 2011, we flew via Brisbane and Hongkong to London, where we took a train to Paris via the underwater tunnel between the two countries. We travelled by bus around in Europe – Paris, Aix-en-Provence, Madrid, Barcelona, Rome and Venice – staying at cheap backpacker hostels, until we finally arrived in Sweden. There we participated in a linguistic conference. I gave a presentation of the languages in Solomon Islands, and Robert informed about Kwaio language. We visited my cousins quite close to the Norwegian border. Robert, as an islander, kept jumping to and fro across the border – a line across the road – enjoying the thought of thereby changing country! This time we returned eastwards via Singapore and Port Moresby.

It was interesting to see the so-called developed part of the world through Robert's eyes. He was interested in trains and in the cruise ship to Finland, with its fancy restaurants and night clubs – quite different from the 'crammed-full rust-buckets' in Solomon Islands. He was fascinated by the bridge between Denmark and Sweden – one of the longest in Europe – and by the railway between Great Britain and France – the longest underwater tunnel in the world.

We celebrated the two main Swedish festivities Walpurgis Night and Midsummer among friends; Robert being mesmerized by the light summer nights. In London, we saw – as tourists must – Buckingham Palace and London Zoo (with the tasty fish!). But he was shocked to see so many homeless people sleeping in the street, and so many beggars. 'Don't they have a *family* and *land*?' was his question. In Fiji, he felt ill at ease seeing Fijians – his wantok Melanesians – offering to polish his shoes.

Robert was not too impressed by the world overseas. He, as well as I, found life artificial and stressful, and we were both eager to return home as soon as possible. But he is content with having *been* overseas, which gave him broader perspectives, and we have a lot of fun when remembering and referring to places and events during our two trips.

Both of us have the same impression when we, or I, pay a visit to Brisbane: a high stress level, hurry, hurry. This in spite of the fact that Brisbane is regarded the most relaxed town in Australia.

Tourist life

During the following years, I would receive guests from other countries. Some were delighted, others hit the ceiling because of lack of facilities (e.g., tap water, electricity, indoor toilet, washing machines...) and yet others were in between these two reactions.

When showing them around, I became a tourist myself and visited places I perhaps would not have seen otherwise. The sights of Honiara are quickly done: Mendana Avenue up and down, Central Market, National Museum, Art Gallery, Parliament House, Botanical Garden, US War Memorial. The last-mentioned is situated just above our house and is maybe nothing special to see, unless you are interested in war history. But the view, the view. The wanderer who has puffed up the hill and hot road (there are buses, though) gets her or his reward. Towards the north-east is the whole of Chinatown with them sea in the background and the Mataniko River as a blue, sometimes brown, ribbon in the bottom. South-west are the soft green hills of Guadalcanal. In the evenings, people, especially youths, gather there and enjoy the sunset and the evening breeze.

Brenda from New Zealand and I met in Tonga, and now she came to visit me. Wojtek and Ania arrived in Solomon Islands from Poland to explore the myths about giants and UFOs in the interior of Guadalcanal. Those myths are depicted in the book *Solomon Islands' Mysteries* by Marius Boirayon. Bob from Germany was his own tourist. We have kept in contact. Robert and I stayed with him in Berlin, and during his frequent visits in Honiara, he stays with us. With his sunny personality he makes friends with everyone; he absorbs Melanesian mentality like nobody else.

My Norwegian travel companion Tore came to visit me. We went to Auki and from there to the little Auki Island some distance out from the harbour.

Then came some friends from Sweden: Barbro, Mechtild, Eva and Björn R. Barbro and I tried to snorkel at Bonegi Beach, but the waves were too strong and high. Luckily, we found the lovely Mbonehe River with cool fresh water from the mountains. We went to Savo, west of Honiara, a little island with many attractions: a volcano, hot springs, 'egg fields' of the megapode bird, dolphins jumping and following the boat, snorkelling... We stayed at Sunset Lodge, and of course we saw the sunset. And relaxed in the hammock with a sunset drink.

Mechtild, Eva and I went by motorboat to the modest Maravagi Resort on Nggela Islands in Central Province. It is a small-scale resort, locally owned, with beautiful clear waters for snorkelling. There was actually nothing to do but relax, stroll and snorkel. After this, we visited the island of Tetepare, a nature reserve known for its fantastic wildlife. In just a few days we saw monitor lizards, coconut crabs, opossums, giant turtles, dolphins, dugongs, crocodiles...

Back in Honiara, we strolled through the wild Botanical Gardens. We had just read the above-mentioned book about giants and UFOs, which partly takes place inside the Botanical Gardens. Even though we – *of course* – don't believe in any of these mysteries, we still thought we saw giants behind every bush and jumped when a banana plant fell down with a crash, maybe thrown by a giant...

With Björn R. I went to Solomon Peace Memorial Park, also called the Japanese War Memorial. Later, I met him in Stockholm.

And then there were some sailing boats with a Swedish crew and finally a Swedish man from Australia, Björn S. But he is not a tourist but works at IFC/World Bank in Honiara. We meet sometimes and keep up our language.

As well as all sightseeing and experiences there was also one or two Solbrew at Mendana Hotel, a dip in the pool at Honiara Hotel and a glass of white wine in the shade at Coral Sea Resort. And panpipes at King Solomon Hotel. This is not something I would otherwise do, not so often anyway.

Compensation

There was a discussion going on in the yard. It happens frequently and almost always for the same reason: A boy and a girl have run away together. This is a matter for both their families, and now the girl's family demands compensation. Negotiations begin; the kastom system starts to operate.

The discussion goes on in a friendly atmosphere, with some joking and laughing – the parties are aware of the delicate situation. It is absolutely out of character with Melanesian culture to show aggressive behaviour or to lose your self-control. If one of the parties is very upset or threatening, the others will postpone the discussion. At last, the conflict is solved when the boy's family pays some thousand dollars in compensation. The sum depends partly on the girl's role in the whole affair; if she has followed the boy of her own will or if she has been forced.

Premarital sexual relations can thus become an expensive affair for the boy. He will either be forced to marry the girl or pay compensation. It doesn't happen so much to the girl. She is usually welcome back. She may risk a bad reputation if she repeats the same history, and much depends on her own behaviour. If a baby is born, it is taken care of by the girl's family. 'You are supposed to have children anyway, sooner or later', they seem to reason. The situation of unwed mothers in this country is relatively good compared to many other parts of the world.

Compensation is also paid to resolve other types of conflicts, e.g., land conflicts, pig thefts, breaching of some taboo, defamation, unruly or abusive behaviour – yes, improper behaviour in general. The consequence is always of economic nature, with cash, i.e., with dollars, or with traditional means, i.e., shell money. A relative of ours must pay $600 because his wife had sworn at someone. Even crimes can be made good by compensation. At a case of knifing the victim demanded a sum of $1,000 from the perpetrator. The relatives of the perpetrator contributed, and the police were never involved, despite this being a serious criminal offence. More severe crimes are handled by police and justice. The country has thereby two parallel judicial systems, although only one is recognized by law.

Kastom and wantok

The word 'kastom' is heard everywhere in Melanesia, as well as 'wantok'. Kastom can, as previously mentioned, stand for everything from the time before colonization and influence from the outside world. And since Melanesia is characterized by a great ethnic and linguistic diversity, language has become a source of identity and has led to the wantok system.

In practice, the word wantok is limited to biological relatives, family members, at least for larger ethnic groups. One has obligations to help a wantok with food and housing and can, in turn, count on help another time. This system is found in several less-industrialized cultures in the world, not the least among Solomon Islands' neighbours, Australian Aboriginals.

The wantok system used to make everyone about even in the past, when everybody was living under the same conditions, in villages with subsistence economy. But in our monetary economy, the system can lead to an absurdly skewed situation. For example, a family living in the capital is obliged through the wantok system to house and feed an unlimited number of wantoks for unlimited time. Instead of harvesting or fishing free food and picking firewood in the bush, they have to buy everything, and it can be quite expensive in the long run. Some wantoks staying with relatives in town contribute to the household in the form of a sack or two of kumara from the village; others don't.

As a member of a family, any individual has thus the right to be cared for. To deny a family member this would be like denying one's own child. It doesn't matter what personal opinion one has, what one wants or does not want; it is something one has to accept.

Persons within politics or the legal system, too, have wantoks and obligations to them, which sometimes may collide with the principle that everyone should be judged equally. The system works as a strong social network but may also hinder the development of a society with justice and equality across the ethnic and linguistic borders.

The word 'wantok' has in our times of increased internationalisation been given a further meaning: anyone you identify with, more or less. Two persons from Vanuatu, but from different ethnic groups, may call themselves wantoks if they meet outside Vanuatu. And one from Vanuatu and one from Fiji may regard themselves as wantoks if they meet outside the Pacific.

The Colonial Ghost

I have been welcomed and accepted into the family from the first meeting. And in town. Never one single negative reaction from anyone. Ever. But I am both inside the community and outside. That first time in Fousisigi, after the slaughter of a pig on Christmas Eve, I was served separately inside the house, while the others were sharing the pig outside. It was meant to honour me, but I missed the joy of a common meal, and it hurt.

Later in the village, I was again served on a separate plate, a little more stylish than the others. Actually, not so much because I was a 'White' and a foreigner but because I was a temporary guest from town. Dignitaries, such as visiting chiefs from other villages, are also served separately. Robert, too, was served separately. He liked it. But I don't. I don't want to be a dignitary; I want to be a family member. 'Equality-Sweden' is deep inside me. I tried to explain how I felt, and the young ones understood. Now, some years later, it seems to be solved. That is to say, I got my way and share a plate with the others.

And when I am climbing up to the gardens in East Kwaio, or digging up kumara and carrying it down in sacks. And when I am peeling kumara. And when I am feeding the pigs. I try to tell my relatives that my grandparents were farmers, that my cousins had pigs, that I myself had a garden plot. Then they laugh, the way you do when you are convinced that somebody is lying but let it go for the sake of peace. And when I am travelling in a truck and everybody is sitting in the tray, and the driver insists that I must sit in the cabin. Or at events where hundreds of people are standing up and somebody brings me a chair.

I complain to Robert. He objects,

'But it's natural to treat people from other countries better! It's our culture. Don't they do that in Sweden?'

'What...hmm...yes, of course.' (If only he knew... But I haven't the heart to tell him about all the racism and xenophobia in my country of birth.)

Robert finds my reaction strange. But I insist. In addition, modesty is a Melanesian virtue, so I can't be that wrong.

Anyway, this view of 'Whites' may take on almost comic proportions. One day, when I was cutting beans, a neighbour woman passed by.

'You work as a real Solomon woman now,' she said approvingly. I smiled, because I understood that it was meant as a compliment, but also asked also why.

'Because you are *cutting beans*!'

Although the islanders here have accepted me with open arms, it is as if they don't really believe I can do the tasks they perform. I am often met with, not suspicion, absolutely not, but *disbelief*; I am not expected to be able to sweep the floor, not peel kumara, not gut fish, not wipe little baby bottoms.

It is not I who create this alienation. It is the image of 'Whites'. From where does this image originate? Very few Solomon Islanders have access to TV or video, few remember the colonial era before independence 1978, and few have been to Honiara and seen the foreign experts, business leaders and aid workers. The volunteers who reach the rural areas live a simple life. Still, 'Whites' are considered as some kind of half-gods who cannot do anything practical. Correspondingly, many Solomon Islanders are convinced that they themselves cannot do anything theoretical, hence the need for so many consultants and experts. This is the other side of the same coin. The Colonial Ghost.

Our German Rasta friend Bob had the same experience of being treated as such a half-god, especially when he was peeling kumara or chopping firewood. But he can be a little mean sometimes. When he was met with surprise because he was peeling kumara, he said dead seriously that yes, in Europe they have a special kind of potato, which comes out from the ground directly peeled and washed.

A Solomon woman stated to me,

Big daddy lo heaven hem high – she pointed upwards – *then white man* – she pointed one step down – *then black man* – she pointed almost to the ground. Her own (Solomon) pastor had told her this.

A Solomon man stated that God had sent the white man as an example for the black man. Scary. Since I know that the Bible is considered as the most authoritative source of truth, I countered,

Jesus talem evribodi seim seim, 'Jesus says that everybody is the same.'

There are fundamental values and needs one cannot compromise – something which all immigrants know – and my fundamental need is to be treated equally, neither higher nor lower. Already as a child, I knew that all human beings were of equal value. It never occurred to me that one could judge others by skin colour, ethnicity or religion, and it came as a surprise that some people actually do.

With all of this, most certainly, a feeling of alienation and isolation can sometimes creep up on me. I have no problems whatsoever identifying myself with isolated immigrant women in Sweden. That is to say, not those who come together with their families and fellow countrymen but those who come one by one, married to a Swedish man, to a (small) town.

Sometimes, when it all feels uphill, I remind myself that I am happy as long as I have a coconut palm in sight. And I look up and see there! Always a coconut palm.

A death

One man, Ben, who called Robert his 'uncle' and who was called 'uncle' by Robert, too, had been ill for a long time and was admitted in National Referral Hospital. His family members gathered, sat with him, fanned him, prayed for him. His condition quickly worsened, and he died after a short time, leaving behind his wife and six children, of which the youngest was new-born.

According to kastom, his body was taken by his family for a wake, in this case by an older brother, who had a big house outside Honiara. He was the one who would take care of the widow and the children. All relatives staying in town gathered. Robert joined them the same day, and I the next day. By that time, around fifty persons had gathered on the lawn. Inside the house, the deceased was lying in an open coffin, which was decorated with silk flowers and beautiful lavalavas. His mother and his widow with the new-born at her breast and the other five children were sitting by the coffin. The mood was sorrowful; some were weeping quietly. The mother asked me to take a photo of the deceased. He had changed physically; his swollen skin had taken a black-bluish colour and he did not look like the lively man I remembered. I did what they asked and sat with them for a while.

Outside, more and more persons were gathering, and at last there were some hundreds inside and around the house. They were sitting, walking, chatting quietly. Some talked about the deceased and wept. Some men were tying a canvas to some trees as a cover, in case of rain. Those who could had given rice, noodles, tayio, coconuts and Coffeemix to the family, and now some women were boiling the rice and grating the coconuts. When the food was ready, everybody ate.

According to kastom, relatives and friends sleep with the family the first nights. So the wake continued in small groups during the day, evening and night. At night, those who were still awake were praying and singing in chorus: Christian songs and traditional Kwaio songs. We slept from time to time, Robert with men and I with some women on the lawn. We were lying on a big sleep mat woven of pandanus leaves. Towards the morning it was chilly, so we covered ourselves with another mat. But there never was any rain.

I liked Ben's old mother very much. She asked me to print the photo of the deceased in the coffin and give her. Then she brought the photo she had peeled off his driving license and asked me to enlarge it and print it too, which I of course did. These two photos were the only ones she had of her son.

A few days later, the deceased was taken by a chartered airplane to his home village in Malaita, where he would be buried. The cost for the transport was shared between the relatives. Even after the body has been flown to his village, the closest relatives stayed with the family until ten days have passed.

The ten days end traditionally with a new overnight gathering, and after one hundred days, the deceased is again honoured by a gathering. Food is served, but *not pork*, which is reserved for happy events. Many male relatives don't shave during these hundred days.

Later, there were some other tragic deaths. A young father of three and a close relative of ours, then a young woman who died in childbirth, a two-year-old boy who drowned. And old people die when their time has come. Everyone is honoured with a wake and are generally buried in the home village except a few who, for different reasons, are put to rest in Honiara city's burial site.

Robert and I, too, were once hosting a wake, being a family's only representatives in Honiara. Our house is small, so there was only room for twelve persons: four adult women (including me) sharing two single mattresses in the big room, five young unmarried girls sharing one double mattress crossways in the small room, and three men (including Robert) sleeping on woven mats on the veranda.

People avoid mentioning the name of the one who died. Instead, they call her or him 'the deceased' or 'the body'.

A church wedding

Wedding day! Robert and I had been invited to a *marrit*, 'marriage, wedding'. In front of the little stone church, the bride Janet was waiting with her father, three bridesmaids and three marshals. The ceremony began with a speech by the pastor, a man with soft authority and the gift of speech. The bridegroom Alec entered; the bride was handed over ceremonially. The obligatory question was answered with an 'I do'; the ring for the bride, brought in on a white silk cushion, was put on; the couple kneeled and were blessed, and then they were married.

The couple had met at Solomon Islands College of Higher Education (SICHE), where they were studying. They are both from Malaita but from different regions and thus speak Pijin among themselves.

Outside the church, the thus united families arranged themselves for photographs, and all the guests – that is, the whole village – filed before the couple, shook hands and wished them good luck. The bridegroom wore a black suit, white shirt and turquoise silk bow tie, sweating streams, and the bride wore a white silk dress. The turquoise colour re-appeared in the maids' dresses and the marshals' waist ribbons.

After some time of us mingling, we left our presents on a mat in the yard. And, although I should know better, I breached the protocol a little. While the other guests kept their gifts in the plastic bags they carried them in, I took out my packet. I wanted to honour the bridal couple with a nice wrapping. But, as previously mentioned, it is not a part of Melanesian culture to show off gifts, and that is just what I did. I guess I have made some more minor mistakes like that, but it would be unrealistic if I hadn't. As Wendy, my New Zealand friend in Vanuatu, says,

'The longer you live in a culture, the more you risk making mistakes.'

Afterwards, we were invited to a buffet table, where a whole motu-baked pig was enthroned, together with traditional dishes. The specially invited guests – some twenty among which were Robert and I – were asked to pick our food first, and then the rest of the village. The wedding cake, shaped like a heart and decorated with icing, was cut. More speeches. There was no music during the whole wedding.

The bride gave a speech and thanked everybody who had come. She was now wearing her new jewellery, which was a part of the bride price: a headband and a large number of long necklaces.

Bride price is a controversial question, and many church leaders and educated families boycott it. The groom can claim that the bride is his property, since he has 'bought' her. On the other hand, the bride's family feel the need to claim compensation for the loss of the girl. Daughters mean income, which makes new-born girls just as welcome as boys.

After the wedding, the families of the bride and the groom respectively gave each other a live pig. One may call it a zero-sum game. *But gifts are not meant to increase the property of any party but to strengthen the friendship.* It makes me see Swedish Christmas presents in a new light.

A kastom wedding

Abi and Jack were getting married in East Kwaio. Abi is Robert's niece and a nurse. Jack, a carpenter, was her fiancé of a few years.

It wasn't yet sure if the wedding would take place during Christmas as planned. Jack's father had died just a few months earlier, and nobody was in the mood for a wedding feast. He had become seriously ill and died after two weeks in hospital, only 55 years old. Nobody could really tell the cause of death, but he had been suffering from severe diabetes and liver inflammation (no alcohol consumption). There were rumours that he had been poisoned by sorcery. Rumours like that are common when somebody dies suddenly and at a relatively young age.

But this occasion at Christmas suited so well, since all relatives were gathered. The next suitable occasion would maybe not come until one year later, and that was definitely too long for the bridal couple. Jack's father, who knew he had weak health, had expressed clearly that even if something happened to him, he wanted the wedding to take place as planned. Thus, the widow, Jack's mother, decided to fulfil the plans. Her late husband's relatives turned against her, saying that she dishonoured his memory. But now it was going to happen anyway.

This was a real Kwaio wedding. On the very day, all possible relatives came paddling to the groom's village. His relatives had collected the bride price, in the shape of shell money.

As mentioned, Langa Langa and Kwaio are the main two regions that make shell money, but the Kwaio ones are used only among Kwaio themselves. Thus, one-meter-long strings of reddish-brown seashell disks tied together in bundles, *ban'au*, were hung on a bamboo rack to be admired, and indeed, the shell money is very beautiful in its gracious design. After a good deal of mingling, the formal part of the wedding began. The bridal couple's leading relatives welcomed everybody in speech after speech. Then, the bundles of shell money were counted: ...20, 30...50, 60...The counting ended at 70.

One string costs $100; thus a bundle of six strings costs $600. Seventy bundles mean $42,000. The price of a better second-hand car. The parents of the bride declared their acceptance of the sum. The bundles were taken down, carefully put in plastic bags and kept by the bride's parents. They will indeed be useful, since the bride has three unmarried brothers.

The bride's mother told me that once, the bride price for her had reached 120 bundles. Proudly she added that it was the highest price somebody among the Kwaio had ever paid for a bride. And she has been worth it: has given birth to five sons and one daughter and is now organising the household and daughters-in-law with authority. That wedding was arranged by the couple's parents.

But back to the wedding of today. If it had been really traditional, the bride's mother told me, the bride would be sitting in a room while the others were preparing the festivities. Nude of course, as unmarried girls traditionally are. When everybody had agreed on the price, the bride's mother would go to her and give her the blue apron that only married women may wear. She would decorate her with the shell money.

After this, the bride would go out for everybody to see and admire her, and she would take part in the feast.

The feast, yes – it could begin. Relatives had brought food from all the surrounding villages: around ten live pigs, several rice sacks at 20 kg, mountains of kumara and other root crops. The pigs were carried ashore from the canoes. Tied and hysterical with death agony, they were screaming heartbreakingly like only pigs can do until the very end: a fast knife stab in the chest. Now, their bodies were washed in the river, charred over open fire, scraped and cut up into large pieces in no time. The feast participants wrapped the pieces in banana leaves and baked them in a pre-built motu. The meat, as well as the rice and the root crops, were shared between the different feast participants, who in that way had food for several days ahead. Some parts of the meat were chopped in small pieces and put into bamboo canes, which were heated in the fire.

It is the relatives of both the bride and the groom who together give the feast and bring the food, usually in the village of the boy. And now, the food is shared with the same relatives. In other words, it is even. And '...gifts are not meant to increase the property of any party but to strengthen the friendship', as previously mentioned.

Nobody had brought any presents (since this is a foreign invention), and there was no music. The feast was about food, food and talk, talk.

So this was a very successful wedding, (almost) totally according to tradition. Relatives, shell money, pigs. *Only the bridal couple was missing!* They had unfortunately not been given leave from their work in Honiara. But it wasn't so important. They were already living together for some time. The main thing was that the families had concluded their agreement.

The fact that both bride and groom are absent and the wedding is still valid, that was news to me. But you learn as long as you live.

A couple can, as mentioned, live together without being married. That is to say, without fulfilling the shell money payment. At least for a short time. If it is for a longer time, they are looked down upon by many: *he* is a skinflint, and *she* gives herself for free.

A kastom wedding is without any judicial ceremonies but with the firmer social commitment. It is legally valid also in the other countries of Melanesia, since those share the same system.

A third wedding

And yes, Robert and I have stayed together. When we met, we were both prepared to dive head-first into unknown waters and try, try. Robert was thinking carefully. He had seen too many mixed marriages end when the foreign partner went back to her or his country for a 'temporary visit' but never returned. I was not thinking at all.

After my arrival in 2007, we lived together for a few months before we were united in a kastom marriage. But Robert never paid any bride price. First, my family were not present. Second, he reasoned like this, with a glint in his eye: As there is no bride price system in Sweden, and since he claimed to 'respect my culture', he wanted to follow Swedish tradition. This would surely be considerably cheaper for him! His relatives felt a little sorry for me and meant that I must have something, so they gave me a piece of jewellery which had been in their family for generations. It was a necklace of very finely polished shell disks and dolphin teeth, which I am very proud of. A kind of symbolic bride price. I wear it always, and it is always met with admiration. Anyone can identify it as a traditional Kwaio piece of jewellery.

Also, we did not have a big feast. Since we were about to go to Sweden, we postponed this part until later. And really, some months after our return, many relatives happened to be gathered in Koa Hill at the same time. A pig was slaughtered, and the feast took place.

A memory: In Sweden we met my two cousins, Eva and Ulla, and Robert gave them shell necklaces as a symbolic bride price. The necklaces were much admired, and somebody asked how they got them. Their reply was: 'We sold our cousin!'

Some time after our kastom marriage we were wed legally at Central Magistrate Court, a formal ceremony in ten minutes. But even without fancy arrangements, a happier bride has never been seen!

PART III: EVER
           AFTER

PART III: EVER AFTER

Dynamics and peace

New house

The two books upon which this new one is based were published in 2008 and 2011, respectively. Now it is 2020. What has happened in those years? Sometimes I have mentioned changes here and there in the running text, but here come more.

For my personal part, there have not been any dramatic changes. Robert and I are still married. We are still living in Koa Hill, Honiara. We still have only solar panels, but we have applied for electricity and been promised 'maybe next week' (for the last two years...). Relatives still come and stay with us for long periods, according to kastom. But the children around us have become teenagers, and the teenagers have become adults with children of their own, and it has all happened so eerily quickly.

One change on the personal level is Robert's work. Since he was discontented with his working hours as a bus driver, he managed to buy a decrepit car and drive his own taxi. He repaired it, sold it and bought a better one. Through the years, he repeated these activities – even with two minibuses – and now we have a brand-new car! As a matter of fact, he is working more now, but it has given us a more regular schedule, and most of all, he is his own boss.

Another change on the personal level is the new house. The first house, the little pretty palm leaf house of 18 m² I moved into in 2007, has been pulled down. I loved it very much, but palm leaves are not very durable, and the house was leaking. We tried to repair with pieces of cardboard, but at last we had to give up and pull it down.

Robert had always wanted a permanent house, built with timber or tin. I resisted strongly and wanted a leaf house, to maintain the local culture, and we went on and on about it... At last he got his way. The winning argument was that leaf houses have to be repaired over and over again. We found a job lot of red corrugated tin at a reasonable price. So carpenters began to build the new house beside the old one, and by Easter 2019 we could move in. It looks like a Swedish dream with its red walls and white window frames. It is bigger than the first one but still relatively small, 24 m². At the moment, there are five of us living here: the two of us and three young girls, who are studying in Honiara. But from time to time, there are 10-12 persons staying.

A clear advantage: The view from the old house was covered by our banana plantation, a green, compact wall. The new house is incredibly hot inside but has a wonderful view over Guadalcanal's wuthering heights.

Photo 27

Economy and paradoxes

Robert's salary as a bus driver was good – $4,000 a month – but the conditions were not the best, as previously mentioned. One week he was working evening shift and another week morning shift. In between he came back home at midnight and then had to get up again at 4.30 a.m. Further, in the beginning he had two scheduled free days a week, but then they were *removed*. Even though his employer accepted that he and the other drivers took free days sometimes, he was *expected to work seven days a week*.

Jimmy didn't have any better situation. For some time, he worked as a day-time security guard at Honiara High School for a paltry $500 a month. He was free on Sundays. But then his schedule was changed to night-time. And then he was not free *one single night*. The employer argued that 'he was free every day'. And finally, his 60-year-old body could not take any more, and he had to give notice and become unemployed.

The conditions in town with a monetised economy are different from the countryside, which relies on a subsistence economy. One kg of rice costs $10, but many people buy sacks at 10 or 20 kg, which is relatively cheaper. Rice is imported and considered to be fairly cheap. Tayio for $5 is very popular. The waters around Solomon Islands are teeming with tuna, and the canning of tuna into 'tinned tayio' is certainly one of the main industries. *But the imported tayio from Thailand is cheaper, and people will of course buy the cheaper one.* How can it be cheaper?

However, if you want a whole fish, you pay c. $30 for a fish for four persons. Fresh, caught by local fishermen. Salted fish, caught by foreign trawlers, cost only c. $10. It has been salted for up to half a year and may give you a rash or boils, even after soaking in fresh water. *But since it is much cheaper, most people buy it and accept the rash and boils.* It is often the only alternative for city folk to eat fish. Robert and I boycott salted fish. We would rather eat kabis more often and fresh fish less often.

PRICE EXAMPLES 3, 2020, SBD	
Rice 20 kg $150	Pig live $1,000-3,000
Tayio tin $5-10	Petrol 1 litre $13
Tuna fresh $30	T-shirt $35
Tuna salted $10	Cheap mobile $120
Eggs 10-pack $35	School fee secondary school
Chicken wings 2 kg $65	for I year $2,000

This is the height of cynicism. How ironic is it that these proud fisher people must eat unhealthy salted fish? In their own country?

I have not yet grasped these paradoxes.

Finally, if you are keen on pork, the price of an adult pig is $1,000-3,000, depending on size. That is, alive; you have to slaughter it yourself. The meat is enough for 10 households for two to three days.

As previously mentioned, a good salary for a professional driver is $4,000 a month. For low-income employment as a security guard, the salary is only $400-600 a month, and for a housekeeper or shopkeeper even less. This is after tax deduction – the employer pays tax in advance.

But many employers won't follow these instructions, and the employees don't feel that they are in a position to demand their rights.

However, there are some other factors to consider when it comes to private economy of the Solomon Islanders. The housing costs are generally low. Those who have built their own house pay nothing, possibly $100 per year for the land tenancy. Those who rent a simple house pay $300-2,000 per month. The rent for a luxury house with indoor water and WC may cost $5,000 and up. There are even higher, outrageous rents of $50,000-70,000 per month, but only a few expatriates can afford that, or – if they are sent out as advisors – their employers in their home country.

Solomon families are big, with many mouths to feed (but also with many hands for work). There are no child allowance payments or other social benefits. However, there is the National Provident Fund (NPF), a kind of private pension system, from where you can withdraw money once you retire from work. But most people rely on their family. Economically strong citizens in town are helping their family members in rural areas with purchased goods. And family members in rural areas are sending agricultural products. Sacks with rice go in one direction and sacks of kumara in the other.

The Big Flood

The clouds had gathered during the morning. First, it was all still. There was no wind, but then it started to blow, and within two minutes the tropical rain was pouring down. The family raced around like headless chooks to save the almost dry laundry. Everybody was hiding indoors, in the dwelling house or in the kitchen. It was a torrential downpour pelting down; it was gushing from the roof; would it never stop? *Is* there that much rain? Then it ceased, just as suddenly as it began.

It is rainy season, and all of you who have been to the tropics know what it means. Laundry which never dries, a musty smell of mould everywhere. Sometimes it is pouring down non-stop for days. During long periods like that, it may cause problems with the laundry. If it is raining more than one week, the washed but still wet clothes begin to smell. The clothes must be absolutely dry when you take them indoors. The slightest damp makes the black mould spread, and the clothes are covered with black spots, which will never, ever vanish. The same thing happens when the clothes are soaked for more than 24 hours.

If the rain is heavy, roads lie under water, bridges are flushed away. During some rainy seasons, we have not been able to leave the house. We normally cross the river with the raft, but in case of heavy rain, the current is too strong. There is a path on land, but it is steep and muddy. Luckily, we have stored rice and tayio. Luckily, too, we have not been hit by any cyclone like other island nations, e.g., Samoa, Cook Islands and French Polynesia. Solomon Islands is situated in some kind of pocket, where cyclones (mostly) pass on both sides but not in the middle.

Heavy rain during rainy season is something normal; that is why it is called rainy season. But in April 2014 the rain caused a flood, the worst within living memory. It was pouring nonstop for five days, and soon it was getting serious. It was raining and raining, and the Mataniko River below our house was running wilder and wilder. The water was surging forwards, pulling away tree branches and rubbish. One desperate man had fallen in the water and was thrown around like a stick but managed to rescue himself to the shore. If not...

Palms were being torn up by the roots and flushed away. Two small children were torn from their mother's arms and drowned. Parked cars were turned upside down and pulled along with the water, and look! A two-story building was just lifted up and sailed away, with people inside. The grass slopes several metres above the river lay under the water. The small bridge in Vara Creek collapsed first, then the large Mataniko Bridge. The water was rising and rising; now it had reached the pig pens in Upper Koa Hill. Neighbours came rushing and managed to get the pigs out before the pens might fall apart and be swept away with the stream.

The children who were staying with us were hysterical. We set off in a hurry up the hillside to the Skyline Road, where we stood mesmerized, watching the scenario. (For three days we were evacuated in a guest house. That guest house and a nearby school were housing everybody from Koa Hill, some of them for a whole month.)

Now, on this day of the Big Flood, once the water had risen five meters, it stopped. After a few hours it began to go down, and a few days later it had reached its normal level. Nobody in Upper Koa Hill was injured and no dwelling houses or pig pens were destroyed. Only the toilets were flushed away.

However, not everybody was that lucky. In Lower Koa Hill and in other parts of Guadalcanal the violent rain had led to landslides; whole villages had been swept away. The government declared a State of Emergency. The results were 25 deaths and 12 missing. One of those missing, a young boy, was a relative of ours. His body was washed ashore on a distant island two weeks later. By then it was so decomposed that they could only identify him from his tattoos.

I was never afraid that the water would reach and flush away our house, since I saw it slowing down long before that level. But I was afraid of landslide. We live on a slope, and there were several cases of landslide around. I saw in my imagination how me and my near and dear would be buried under tons of mud. And a landslide may take place many days after a heavy rain. Now, every time there is a veritable pour-down, I feel panic...

Afterwards, the National Disaster Management Office carried out investigations. They found that it was not so much the violent raining that caused the serious flooding as it was the intensive logging by foreign companies. The strong trees that would have held the soil and the rushing water had been cut down, and the roots themselves were not able to stop it. Besides, all the logs had been piled up and formed a giant dam, which had now burst and let loose the water.

Alcohol and other drugs

On Saturday mornings a gang, mostly men and a few women, meet on the other side of the river opposite our house, in Vara Creek. They sit on the grass drinking the homemade spirits, *kwaso* (not to be confused with cassava pudding, *gwasu*), and playing loud music. They begin early, around six in the morning. Around eight, they are getting noisy, and by noon, when the sun is high, they have blacked out. They sleep in the spot all day. In the evening they begin again. Sleep again and start again on Sunday mornings.

Alcohol is a new substance introduced by the colonizers. The indigenous population has not yet built up any biological tolerance against alcohol the way they have in Europe with its thousands of years of alcohol traditions. Also, Solomon Islands are in a period of transition between old and new, between subsistence economy and monetised economy, between the security in the village and the town's attractions and unemployment. Frustrated, people escape into the wonderland of the alcohol haze. And alcohol evokes aggression, compared to the use of kava in the rest of the Pacific, which has a tranquilizing effect. The consequences of alcohol are totally devastating, socially, economically and medically, both for the individual and for the country.

The alcohol mentioned is the country's own strong beer, Solbrew and SB. But cheaper and more hard-hitting is the illegal kwaso. In the outer settlements of Honiara, the stills are chugging. The police are doing continuous patrols, but the producers pop up at new places.

Lately, there has been an increase in the cultivation and smoking of marijuana. Like kwaso, marijuana is illegal, but it is a plant and almost impossible to find in the jungle that encloses the settlements.

The only indigenous drug is the peaceful betel nut, but it has other disadvantages, as previously mentioned.

Violence

On the radio, the bomb bursts: According to a report by UNICEF, Solomon Islands is one of the worst countries in the world for domestic violence, together with Uganda, Somalia, Colombia and Papua New Guinea (Uganda being one of my favourite countries too!). I cannot believe my ears. In some parts of Honiara, yes. But in the country as a whole, in the provinces, in the villages!!?? In my family, and it is big, I have not seen the slightest tendency; it means that the problem must be enormous in other families.

Ruth Maetala at the Ministry of Women, Youth and Children Affairs confirms. Domestic violence, which goes hand in hand with alcohol abuse, is one of the most severe problems of the country. The authorities are well aware of the situation and there are severe punishments for those offenders who are found guilty in the court. However, many will not even get to court, since the victims will not testify – a well-known problem around the world. There are refuges called *Seif pleis*, 'Safe place', for women and children in danger, located in the police compound, and there is an emergency telephone number for victims to call. This number is sent out as mass messages to the mobile phones, and it is pinned on the rice sacks, so women can easily find it.

Domestic violence is not a new phenomenon, and it appears all around the world. But this tremendous increase in Solomon Islands is something new. In the old times among the Kwaio, domestic conflicts were solved in a meeting, where the elderly tried to talk with the involved parties. Punishment could be handed out as a form of economic compensation (where the currency was shell money). Adultery could lead to the death penalty. But at that time, there was no alcohol around.

In Solomon Islands, people are usually not aggressive towards each other. I sense no suppressed aggression from anyone, except from those who are drunk.

Languages in Melanesia

The nations in Melanesia (including Papua New Guinea but excluding Fiji) house a high number of indigenous languages.

Melanesia is the linguist's paradise! The world record is kept by Papua New Guinea with 800-1000 languages, shared between the 8.6 million inhabitants. Vanuatu, on the other hand, has the highest language density in the world, with over 130 languages shared between its 290,000 inhabitants. In Solomon Islands, around 70 languages are spoken by the 690,000 inhabitants, and in New Caledonia around 40, spoken by 285,000.

The situation in the three first-mentioned countries has led to all-encompassing 'umbrella' languages for communication between the language groups, namely: Tok Pisin (Papua New Guinea), Solomon Pijin (Solomon Islands) and Bislama (Vanuatu). (Those three languages are quite similar and can be compared to Danish, Norwegian and Swedish.) They arose during the 19th century, when colonization and blackbirding forced a general shuffling of islanders, who thus had to find ways to communicate. In New Caledonia, the role of an 'umbrella' language was taken by French. In all these countries the ex-colonial languages still have a strong position.

Fiji is an exception to this linguistic diversity. The smaller languages/ dialects, which existed before, have been pushed aside by one dominant dialect, which has nowadays become Standard Fijian, the official language.

As a rule of thumb, one may say that Melanesia is characterized by 'one country – many languages'. This can be compared with Polynesia, which has 'many countries – one language'. The languages in the various Polynesian countries are notably more similar than the various languages within any Melanesian country. Micronesia embraces the principle 'one country – one language'.

The languages in Papua New Guinea belong to the Papuan language family, while the languages in the rest of Melanesia belong to the Austronesian family. Those two language families are not related to each other. A few Papuan languages are spoken in Solomon Islands.

Solomon Pijin

Solomon Pijin, or simply Pijin, is the linguistic cement in Solomon Islands, where the existence of c. 70 separate languages would otherwise rule out communication between the citizens. The official language is English, and Pijin is somewhat looked down upon. It is sometimes called 'broken English' or 'baby English', but nothing could be more incorrect. Pijin is its own language, with the vocabulary mainly from English and the grammar from the local languages. The local languages are members of the Melanesian branch of the Austronesian language family and have a different structure from English. Pijin can be thought of as 'an indigenous language in English clothes', so to say. Between languages, which are similar on the surface, there may exist some so-called 'false friends', i.e., words and expressions which are so similar that you may believe that they really mean the same. But they don't! Some examples:

– *Kilim* doesn't mean 'kill' but 'hit'. 'Kill' is *kilim dae*.

– *Lusim* doesn't mean 'lose' but 'leave, depart'. *Ship lusim Honiara lo 7 p.m.* 'The ship departs from Honiara at 7 PM.' In one song, you can hear: *Wae iuuu luuuuusim miiii?* which doesn't mean 'Why are you losing me?' but 'Why are you leaving me?'

– *Nomoa* doesn't only mean 'no more' but primarily 'only', 'just'. *Mi olraet nomoa.* 'I'm just fine'. Secondarily it means 'no, not'. *Iu hangere? – Nomoa.* 'Are you hungry? – No.' When translating the New Testament to Pijin, there was some embarrassment about Jesus' words to a woman accused of adultery. The Pijin result *Go, and sin no more* was not interpreted as 'Go, and do not sin anymore' but as 'Go, and just sin.'

– *Swim* doesn't only mean 'swim' or 'bathe' but also 'shower'.

– *Opposit* doesn't mean 'opposite' but 'beside'. 'Opposite' is *nader saed* ('another side').

– *Pei* means both 'buy' and 'pay'.

– *Hem/him* means both 'she' and 'he'.

– Possession or belonging is expressed by *blong* or *blo*. *Haus blong/blo mi* means 'house belonging to me', 'my house'.

Pijin is primarily a spoken language. The script has no general standard spelling rules and is many times inconsistent. In its written form, it appears almost exclusively as handwritten signs, for example:

NO TOROWE RABIS LO HIA
'DO NOT THROW (AWAY) RUBBISH HERE'

Another very special example of written Pijin is the charming calendar *Hapi Helti Family* 'Happy Healthy Family', published by Soroptimists International Solomon Islands. Each month they give advice about health and other issues that they want everybody to understand. Here is a campaign encouraging girls to study (May 2009):

Evri gele sud go long skul. Ediukeson hem gud tumas fo fiusa blong olketa gele an blong yumi evriwan.
'All girls should go to school. Education is very good for the future of all girls and of all of us.'

Most Solomon Islanders are (at least) bilingual; speaking their local language and Pijin. In addition, around the border between two ethnic regions, it is common to know the neighbouring language. Together with English, it makes the individual quadrilingual. But still, there are some monolinguals who only know their own local language. It is usually elders who have never been outside their own region.

Non-verbal communication is its own chapter. You answer 'yes' by bending your head slightly backwards and raise your eyebrows. (In Greek, this means 'no'.) When you don't hear what somebody says, you should open your mouth to make her or him repeat (and, as a suggestion, also your ears).

Personal relations are more important than the truth-value of an assertion. Therefore, it may happen that somebody gives you incorrect information, just in order to make you pleased. 'This road goes to the hospital? – Yes.' In addition, it is considered rude to answer 'no' straight out. If you ask somebody to do something, she or he would say that 'it is hard/difficult' or 'maybe later'. Or she or he promises but never fulfils it. Sometimes I have said that something is 'hard', and then the person has looked disappointed. In English it means that something is not easy, but it will be done anyway. This is in contrast to Pijin, where it means that something is totally impossible.

Robert and I always speak Pijin together. It's a very expressive language!

Names, kin terms and ways of addressing

Robert, Andrew, Nancy, John, Rose and whatever they are named. That is how they are named in Kenya and Hong Kong, too. The names are strikingly English and yes, they are remnants from colonial times. The children here get double names, one real, kastom name, and one foreign, 'Christian' name. Rubaka's 'Christian' name is Nancy, and Abi's is Rose. The foreign names don't always fit the sound rules of the indigenous languages and are therefore adapted to them. Thus, Robert is often pronounced 'Robeti' and Andrew 'Anduru'.

Many children have English names because an English-speaking person has named her or him. The name-giver gets some responsibility for the child, in a kind of godparenthood.

The kin terminology in Pijin is affected by the local languages and doesn't always correspond with English, even if they appear similar on the surface ('false friends' again). *Sister* and *brother* can be used in reference to siblings, half or full siblings as well as cousins. Two persons are, in other words, 'sister' and 'brother' to each other if they are offspring of the same parents or *of the parents' siblings*. If needed, one can clarify and differentiate between '*real* sister/brother' and '*cousin* sister/brother'.

In the same way, *mummy* and *daddy* can be used in reference to the biological parents as well as the parents' siblings, especially if the latter have been nursing and feeding the child. Robert once said that he would send a sack of rice by ship 'to my mummy'. 'But isn't she dead??' I asked. But he was referring to Aunty Kwaleka, his father's (real) sister.

There have been anthropological attempts to explain this terminology rationally. Example: If a mother dies, her children are being taken care of by her sister, alternatively by her husband's sister, that is, an aunt. Therefore, it would make it easier for the child if there already is the same word for 'mother' and 'aunt'. For me, this is questionable. First, mothers die in countries with other languages, too. Second, I cannot see any crass reasons of rationality behind the practise. Melanesians simply *regard* 'mother' and 'aunt' as equal. A mother is somebody who has been feeding and raising a child, who later, in her or his turn, will be obliged to support her.

And again, if it is considered important to stress the biological relation, one can clarify with '*real* mother/father'.

If the relation is not quite as close as for *mummy* or *daddy*, there are the words *aunty* and *uncle* respectively. They are used mirror-wise, that is, about both the older generation ('aunt' and 'uncle') and the younger ('niece' and 'nephew'). According to the norm, *aunty* should be used for females and *uncle* for males, but it happens that *uncle* is used also for females. So, *uncle* could refer to a niece or a nephew. And, just like in English, *aunty* and *uncle* can be used, especially by children, to any known or unknown woman or man.

And finally, *granny* can be used both 'upwards', about grandparents (or their siblings or cousins etc.), and 'downwards', about grand-children. Plus all in-laws.

Sometimes, you can hear two persons around the same age call each other 'uncle'. They thus have a biological relation, where someone is sibling or cousin to the other's parent. But you cannot tell easily who is who. A parent's sibling, which thus belongs to the older generation, may be younger in age. Considering the large spans in children's ages within a family, the eldest children may have children of their own before they have a new sibling.

Pijin: *sister* (or *sista*)
= Engl.: sister, half-sister, step-sister, foster sister, female cousin

Pijin: *brother* (or *barada* or *bro*)
= Engl.: brother, half-brother, step-brother, foster brother, male
      cousin

Pijin: *mummy* (or *mami* or *mam*)
= Engl.: mother, step-mother, foster mother, aunt

Pijin: *daddy* (or *dadi* or *dad*)
= Engl.: father, step-father, foster father, uncle

Pijin: *aunty* (or *anti*)
= Engl.: aunt, parent's sister, parent's female cousin

Pijin: *uncle* (or *ankolo*)
= Engl.: uncle, parent's brother, parent's male cousin
= Engl.: aunt, parent's sister, parent's female cousin
= Engl.: nephew, sibling's son, cousin's son
= Engl.: niece, sibling's daughter, cousin's daughter

Pijin: *granny* (or *grani*)
= Engl.: grandparent
= Engl.: grandchild

Few persons call me Ann. Names are considered slightly too intimate. Instead, people are addressed in relation to somebody else. If somebody is a parent, they are addressed in relation to the child, for example *Mummy blong Tome*, 'Tome's mother'. Spouses are often addressed and referred to as *husband/wife blong NN*'.

The most common way of addressing a married Solomon woman is *metron*, 'matron'. *Missis* stands, of course, for 'Mrs', thus a married woman, and a Solomon man can, half-jokingly, talk about *missis blong mi* 'my wife'. But the most common use of *missis* is to address women in a (= an assumed) superior position, e.g. Chinese female store owners and foreign (Caucasian) women. It is a form of address which gives unpleasant associations to the colonial era, the female correspondence to 'master'. It stinks of colonialism.

Yet another means of address coming up lately is *madam* or *ma'am*. This I have heard mostly in Fiji, Samoa and Tonga, but it is beginning to creep into Solomon Islands, especially within the tourism industry and at the university. This is a word, too, that, in my ears, signals superiority and/or distance. Both *missis* and *ma'am* are outdated and a little, how to say it, 'snobbish', without any roots in this relatively equal Melanesian society.

The most intimate and sweet means of address is *mummy* or *mam*. It literally means 'mother' but also 'sweetheart', and it can be used by a loving partner. *Mam* is also used by the drunkards across the river opposite our house, as long as they are in a good mood.

Hello mam! they shout when I come carrying my shopping bags from town, and then I know I can feel secure. *Mam* or *ma'am* – what a tremendous difference.

Otherwise in Koa Hill, where they know me, I am called *metron*. The children call me *aunty*. For relatives, especially male ones, I am called *tabu* or *tambu*, 'taboo'. Derived from 'forbidden', 'sacred', 'untouchable', the word 'taboo' is also used for in-law relatives. Through their marriage they have become forbidden (as a presumptive spouse or sexual partner). Taboos of different sex are subject to social restrictions. For example, they are not supposed to touch each other or sleep in the same room.

Talking about *tabu* and *tambu*; in Melanesian languages, it is common to alternate freely between *b* and *mb*, *d* and *nd*, *g* and *ng*. A woman told me: 'I am a window'.

Among the Kwaio, it is taboo and a deep insult to swear referring to somebody's mouth or teeth. (Think of the English insult 'your big mouth'.) In the 'good old times', it was reason enough to be killed on the spot. Nowadays, this will of course not happen. But even for a modern Kwaio, it is such a strong taboo that she or he may react emotionally to it.

Sibling fights can go like this:

Mother:	'Why did you hit your little brother?'
Big sister:	'He called me "your mouth"!'
Mother:	'Oh, really! Well, in that case...' (scolds little brother)

Robert enjoys talking. Once, when I was sharing a banana, I happened to break it into one big and one small piece. I gave the big piece to Robert with the words 'because you have a big mouth.' He flinched. Then he said, the way he usually does when I have breached some taboo:

'For me it's all right (but I saw that it was not). But be careful when you speak to others.' A mild criticism, but serious.

Focus on age

Sweden is obsessed with age. Everywhere you go you must state your age: at all contact with authorities, when you are interviewed in the street, when you join various internet sites. Therefore, it is such a relief here in Solomon Islands, where fixation with age is non-existent. I mean, age says nothing about my person. It is just as irrelevant as shoe size, bra size or Body Mass Index (BMI).

Here I have never had to state my age, not when opening a bank account, not when seeking medical care (the only time, in my opinion, when it could be relevant). In forms, under Age: .... you just write 'adult'. A few times, a physician has asked me my age orally.

Robert doesn't know his age off the top of his head. Only once he had to state it: when he was signing travel insurance for his journey to Europe. Embarrassed, he asked the female travel agent for help.

'No problem,' she said. 'I know how to calculate it. I don't know my age either, and in addition, *it changes each year. I cannot keep up with this*'. (read: 'I have more important things to think about.'). You take your year of birth and subtract it from the current year. If you don't know your year of birth, you can look in your passport.'

Robert checked his passport, and both bent over a calculator.

Children don't know how old they are. Parents don't know how old the children are, but they know if the child was born before or after the cyclone, etc. And they know their grade assignment at school.

When you want to relate to somebody's age, you compare with a person both know:

'I was just as big as Sirua is now.'

Or you refer to her or his physical development:

'She could not even sit without support when we adopted her.'

'I hadn't even hair under my arms when World War II began.'
(When the war was over, he had both hair under his arms and
a Medal of bravery.)
'You should know better! You are not a child! Your dick has hair!'

People here are trained throughout their life to remember about
others. They know exactly how somebody looks and to whom she or he
is related, what she or he has said and when; they know where and when
an event has happened and can describe a place. I cannot; I forget faces
and names.

Parliament election

One Member of Parliament had been sentenced to prison for corruption.
He must be replaced in a new election. A relative of ours, Alfred Sasako,
ran as a candidate for the position, and I followed the election campaign
with close interest. As politicians usually do, he arranged meetings and
printed pamphlets about himself. But in contrast to Sweden there was
nothing about what he *promised* to do but instead what he *had* done. A
refreshing view! He had for example...

1997	Secured $100,000 funding for Atoifi Adventist Hospital. This helped prevent the Hospital from closing down.
2001	First Solomon Islander awarded scholarship to attend the Executive Program run by the John F Kennedy School of Government, Harvard University, USA
2005	Established the National Agriculture Council Provided assistance to Water supplies (Uru village) Canoe & outboard (Namolaelae) Chainsaw (Olomburi)

and much, much more.

A 'Honourable', i.e., a Member of Parliament, has access to funds
from which the voters can apply for grants, e.g., for school fees, for
transport of a deceased to the home village or for various projects.

Media

Solomon Islands has two daily newspapers: *Solomon Star* and *Island
Sun*.

The country has had radio broadcast for a long time, but its TV
broadcast, Telekom Television (TTV), is relatively new. They have
channels with sports, news, entertainment, commercial and all kinds of
information snippets: smoke warnings, HIV warnings, the importance

of using a condom and the importance of family planning. In addition to TTV, BBC News and Australian News are also available.

Both TV and radio are nice company and a way to learn both Pijin and about the society. Radio news, introduced by panpipes, is presented every hour, in Pijin and English by turns. There is information on how to get bank loans for solar panels and advertisements for, e.g., coconut products and beer. Some typical elements of both information and advertisements are little songs or melodious phrases:

> ♪ *Doim stret samting.*
> *No letim pikinini go smok – o-o.* ♪
> ♪ 'Do something right.
> Don't let children start smoking – o-o.' ♪

There is lots of music by Solomon Islands' innumerable bands. Especially popular is reggae: Melanesian reggae or the artists Lucky Dube or Bob Marley. Regular radio programs each week are: *Helt kona*, 'health corner', with health tips of the day: avoid greasy food, be active, keep warm (!); *Kastom gaden*, 'custom garden', about the importance of composting and ecologically friendly cultivation; and finally, on Saturdays, a music program, where the listeners can call the program and chat, give their greeting to relatives and request a song.

Daily, in the evenings, the English program 'Let the Bible speak' includes reading and commenting on a part of the Bible; later is 'Messages' where, e.g., the announcer informs who has been approved to attend a conference or a workshop and what to bring: Bible, bush knife, mosquito net, plate, spoon. Dates and places for school starts are announced. Still, weeks after the start, the late ones – both teachers and students – continue to be called for on the radio. They risk losing their places if they don't appear. Within Messages on the radio there is the program item *Tok tok sori*, 'Talk of sorry', which consists of reading out the death notices. Even later comes the very important 'Shipping information', telling which ships depart and arrive when and where. Weather reports, of course. On Sundays, only church services and spiritual music all day.

When the Parliament is gathered the debates, held in English, are broadcast live. There is much humming and hawing, repetitions and 'Mister Speaker', and it can be quite slow and deathly boring. The Melanesian communication capability has been strangled by English protocols. *All* Solomon Islanders I have been talking to have snorted at those debates or 'stories'. The contempt for politicians is limitless. But anyway, there *is* a Parliament and a discussion and a political multi-party system; how many countries lack that? Nevertheless, they must have a police helicopter when the Parliament is gathered.

Some remote islands have no newspapers, no radio (not even shortwave), no TV and no mobile coverage. But generally speaking, the media gives a well-composed selection for this dynamic country.

Health and ill-health

Public medical care, including e.g., examinations, ultrasound and medicine, is free in Solomon Islands, even for non-residents. There are plenty of public clinics, both in Honiara and in the provinces, but they are often lacking resources. If one needs to seek medical care at the public National Referral Hospital (popularly called 'Number 9') in Honiara, one must be prepared to stay there up to one day waiting, waiting in the emergency room. There are also private doctors with shorter waiting times, and they charge $100-300. Some have higher prices for expatriates than for locals.

Malaria is a widespread disease here and a common cause of death. The islanders take it somewhat lightly, it seems. Once, I asked Robert if he had had malaria.

'Noo...' he answered, searching his memory, and added, 'Not this year anyway.'

Malaria is curable if it is a mild variety and the victim gets help in time. But I have also seen severe cases, where the disease has affected the brain, because the victims have stayed in villages without roads and without money for boat petrol.

A woman in East Kwaio had been struck by an unusually severe variety of malaria, the one that affects the brain. At night, she was delirious, praying at a furious pace in order to 'cast out the devils', so she said in the morning. At last they could get some petrol, and she was taken in a motorboat to the hospital in Atoifi. She was given treatment but too late; she already had severe brain damage. Concentration difficulties forced her to quit her job as a teacher. Also, she could not take care of her big family, so she left the six children in their father's care and moved back to live with her parents.

Twelve-year-old Andrew had a kind of epileptic attack and was unconscious for three days. He too had got malaria.

Little James was only one month old when he was struck by malaria. His parents hurried to consult the hospital, and after one week's treatment the little boy was all right again. But still, what a beginning of life!

Strangely enough, I have not been affected, touch wood, although I have been here for 14 years and don't take any prophylaxis. In the beginning, I took Chloroquine but I grew fed up and quit, and yet so far, nothing has happened.

The government has introduced a comprehensive campaign: The Project for Strengthening of Malaria Control (PSMC). They work with simple means, and indeed, they have decreased the occurrence. Via free calendars, for example, they spread information about simple actions:

- sleep under a mosquito net (provided free);
- drain bodies of water, e.g., empty tins and flower pots;
- burn rubbish around the house;
- cut and clear bushes;
- keep pigs in pens and prevent them from rooting pits;
- seek medical care immediately if symptoms appear;
- let PMSC's patrols come and spray (free)

Other health problems are respiratory diseases: airway infections, bronchitis, pneumonia and tuberculosis. This is something I associate with the cold humid winter climate in, say, England and definitely not here, where the heat and the chlorophyll brim-full greenery are caressing the respiratory organs. But it is true, and the main cause is supposed to be the smoke from the numerous cooking fires. Another cause is the never-ending sea breeze. And then 'welfare illnesses' like high blood pressure and diabetes.

One Norwegian student at USP was struck by mosquito bites → infection → staphylococcus → hepatitis b → ambulance flight to Australia, in that order.

I, after having been healthy during my whole time here (upset stomach and flu don't count), began to encounter one ailment after another. In this way, I would become acquainted with Solomon medical care more than I wanted.

A wound that never healed brought me to National Referral Hospital for dressing every day for three weeks. While sitting in the waiting room I had plenty of time to study my surroundings. There was a tremendous lack of space. Patients were lying with drips in corridors – yes, even in the waiting room, some secluded with screens, some not. Around each patient there were a number of relatives, who stood, sat or lay around her or him, fanning and trying to decrease the pain. The smell of sweat, urine and sick bodies was notable. Moaning and piercing baby-crying.

Melanesian families are large by tradition. The birth rate in Solomon Islands is very high but declining. It could be explained by active campaigns to bring it down. The authorities are favourable to contraception, and it is very common for women to get themselves sterilized. There are open campaigns, and the little clinic Solomon Islands Planned Parenthood Association (SIPPA) offers counselling, gives medical care, distributes pamphlets on 'child spacing' and much more. Abortion, on the other hand, is illegal. It may also be significant that the doctors are not keen to treat infertility. A couple may get the simple information that *blood blong iutufala hemi no strong*, meaning 'the blood of you two is not strong', and the couple will have to accept that explanation. Well, it is very easy to adopt a child within the family, and the need for biological children doesn't seem so strong. As far as I have seen.

Another campaign is the encouraging of breastfeeding before bottle-feeding. Women breastfeed in public here, which can be compared to the poor woman in England, who was told to leave a bus, because she was breastfeeding her baby. Outside National Referral Hospital, big signs tell that bottle-feeding is not permitted within the hospital area. Very promising. But what will then happen to adopted babies is the question. Those parents will have to hide away, just as breastfeeding women do in other countries.

Photo 28

The authorities are clear-sighted in fighting HIV and AIDS. They run open campaigns on TV and radio, place pamphlets in clinics, distribute free condoms and more, and actually the statistics for Solomon Islands is very low. Many church leaders are negative towards those campaigns. The authorities counter with the slogan:

'If you think knowledge brings harm – try ignorance!'

Many illnesses are cured by kastom medicine, natural medicine. Established medical plants like *noni, moringa, wuruware* and others are sold at the market. One kind of bindweed helps against diarrhoea, stops bleeding and facilitates healing of wounds. It is commonly called 'mile-a-minute', because it grows so fast. Young leaves of pawpaw bring fever down. Coconut water is good for everything. These above-mentioned plants and their effects are known by most islanders. Then there are other plants, which require more specialized knowledge. On our land, we have seven wild medical plants. They look like weed, but they are said to cure toothache, ulcer, chest problems, stomach problems, cancer and more. Robert knows quite a lot, and he is often consulted and asked to produce medicine, either through crushing leaves or boiling leaves or bark.

In 2015-2016 I was seriously ill from a severe chest infection, and I was admitted for three months in the National Referral Hospital in

Honiara. It is a large and modern hospital but has a constant lack of staff and equipment.

Much of the burden falls to the relatives, who fulfil the duties that nurses and assistant nurses would otherwise carry out. The patients have relatives who stay with them all the time, sleep on the floor at night, help the patient to the toilet and to x-rays and other examinations, and feed and wash her or him. Thus, Robert or any of the young girls, who were staying with us, slept every night for three months on the floor beside my bed. The hospital provides bed linen, but most patients prefer their own, as well as their own clothes. The relatives wash the clothes and hang them outside the wards. The patients are served food three times a day but must provide their own plate and cutlery and wash them afterwards. I am almost brought to tears when I think about the luxury of Swedish hospitals and Australian ones, too, as far as I have experienced.

Nobody quite knew what was wrong with me, but I was given blood transfusions and three kinds of intravenous antibiotics. It was a little critical since they did not have any supplies of my blood group, but eventually they got some bags from a private clinic. And in order to be given blood the patient is supposed to have two relatives that donate blood in exchange. (It doesn't have to be the same blood group though.) Robert's niece and nephew stood by. This was a great thing for them, since according to Kwaio kastom, it is taboo to remove anything from the body. This is the case even if it is lifesaving, be it blood donation, amputation or removal of a cancer-affected body organ.

After the first days in the Emergency Ward I was moved to the Surgical Ward and later to the Medical Ward. What was most depressing in the Surgical Ward was all the patients, even young ones, who were moving around in wheelchairs with amputated feet and legs. Diabetes.

The rate of increase of diabetes in the Pacific tops the worlds-rankings. Without resistance, islanders are helpless against the junk food of today: sweet soft drinks, the 'three white killers' (white rice, white bread, white sugar), etc. Hospitals, clinics and newspapers are full of nutritional advice: avoid junk food, sugar and grease, eat and support local food.

The Medical Ward was not much better. I felt as if the germs were dripping down the walls. We were 16 patients in each room, women and men mixed. The light was on all night against the rats, but they came anyway. The fans in the ceiling only worked occasionally. Patients died around me like flies. When somebody had died, the staff screened off the bed to wash the body. The relatives had gathered and, weeping, they followed the body to the morgue. This happened a couple of times a week. I myself was so ill that I was almost surprised to wake up each morning.

Many visitors came to see me, which was very comforting and definitely helped me to recover. Some of them gave me natural medicines: boiled leaves and bark from different medicinal plants. A healer came and rubbed my body with oil and herbs. His explanation for my illness was that somebody had 'thrown the devil upon me'. He described how he had seen it with his 'inner eye'.

A memory: A friend of mine, Mona, came to visit me. In the bed next to mine lay a middle-aged man who was very ill. His skin was greyish, and he was given oxygen. Mona was touched by his state and expressed sympathy. He died later in the evening. Around midnight another man was admitted, around the same age and with similar features. Next morning, Mona returned. She saw the man in the other bed and exclaimed: 'Oh, he looks much better today!' Robert and I could not help smiling. This has become a saying between us: '"He looks much better today", said Mona about the dead man.'

My test results improved. But I became weaker and weaker, and when I was at my worst I was discharged. I could neither stand up nor walk, hardly even sit up. But the infection was gone, and there was a great risk that I could be contaminated by something else. So I was nursed at home, like a baby. Slowly, slowly I recovered my old strength. But probably never quite as before. I lost 17 kg and aged 10 years in two weeks and I have still, after four years, several kilos more to gain. I have been to several check-ups, and everything is ok. The staff know me and are happy for me. Whatever it was – antibiotics, natural medicine, visitors, healing, or my own strong will – it helped. I understand that they expected me to die. But I didn't!

Soap and craft

I have become much more a part of the social life here. First the soap. There is a factory here in Honiara, Kokonut Pacific, which makes products of coconut oil. They used to be situated in the harbour but have now expanded enormously and built a new factory in Lungga, close to the airport. They have become an important export industry and won several prizes. I used to go there and buy soap. They provided paper sheets with instructions on how to make your own soap, and I took one. And in 2012, I began to make soap of coconut oil and sell it on a small scale. I became a member of Solomon Islands Women in Business Association (SIWIBA), which arranges markets, fairs and workshops, and they encouraged me in all sorts of ways.

Then everything happened quickly, one thing after another. The same year, 2012, I went to a language class to improve my homemade Pijin. That course was held at Young Women's Christian Association (YWCA), and in that way, I came into closer contact with them. They needed a volunteer to organise their library, which had been damaged in the ethnic tensions. So that kept me busy for a month or so. I went around to the stores in town and asked for empty noodle cases. I cut them and made them into document binders, where I put books and other documents, altogether five metres of shelving. We called it the 'noodle library'.

The YWCA were delighted. To thank me, they let me participate in any course of my choice, and I chose one in recycling, or specifically, how to cut colourful plastic bags into strips and crochet bags and baskets. At home, I first made a basket for laundry pegs for myself, and then I began to crochet more peg baskets, mobile baskets, beer coolers, bath gloves and other things made of plastic strips. Then I bought fabrics, Pacific designs in lovely colours, and sewed up pillow cases, bags and more. I sold it all together with my soap.

I had been working with my 'brain' for so many years, and now could satisfy my need to work with my 'hands' as well, to be creative in another way. I became a bit of a local celebrity and appeared in newspapers and magazines. Robert and I registered a business, Tropicana Soap & Craft. In 2018, when Solomon Islands celebrated its 40 years of Independence, our business was invited, together with 24 other enterprises, to represent Solomon Islands' business sector. It was an honour and very pleasant.

I used to have my own tent stall in the park of Art Gallery together with many other craft artists: painters, carvers, basket weavers, fabric artists... It was a beautiful park, a true oasis, and I enjoyed it very much. My main product was coconut soap, so I printed and laminated a little kastom story I had seen in Vanuatu, 'The First Coconut', which I displayed in my stall for my delighted customers:

The first coconut: A Melanesian tale
Long ago, on an island in the Pacific Ocean, lived a boy in a cave. He lived there with his mother, who was a big snake. Every day he went to play in a village. When a man asked him where he lived, he told him that he lived in a cave with his mother, who was a snake. Back at home, he told his mother about the man. She was very sad and said that the man would come and find her and kill her.

'Listen my son,' she said, 'if they come and kill me, you must cut off my head and bury it. From my mouth there will grow a big tree. You must care for it, and it will be very useful to you.' Next day, the man came from the village and killed the snake. The boy was very sad, but he did as his mother had told him and cut off her head, and buried it outside the house.

One day, the boy saw a shoot growing out from this place. He cared for it, and one day it had become a tall coconut palm. Finally, it was time for the first fruit. The boy remembered that his mother had told him that it would be very useful, and it was true. He used everything from it, for food, drink, building material, ropes, baskets, brooms, protection from the sun and much more.

If you look at a round shell of a coconut, you will see two eyes and a mouth, resembling the face of a snake, and from its mouth there will always grow a shoot.

From Custom Story from North Efate, Vanuatu, retold by Ann Arika

— — —

...it became the custom that whenever anyone went out sailing, that person would throw a coconut into the sea. This would become food for stranded sailors or fishing people. The nuts also came ashore on other islands and grew there. To this day, the people of the Pacific still throw a coconut overboard whenever they travel by sea and everywhere you go you will see coconut trees growing tall.

From The Coconut Tree: A South Pacific Tale, retold by Sam Warahokia

Then the Government of Taiwan decided to build the new Art and Handicraft Center as a gift to Solomon Islands. The trees were chopped down and the artists thrown into the street, where we raised our stalls on the pavement.

Photo 29

The construction work was delayed, so we kept sitting there for 1½ years, and my already weak respiratory organs were damaged by dust and exhaust fumes. But at last, in 2019 the new centre, a single building with pavilions, was ready to house us. The Prime Minister, The Minister of Culture & Tourism and The Ambassador of Taiwan took part in the opening ceremony with speeches.

Sales decreased rapidly. The centre was so big, and the customers did not find their way to my little pavilion, which I shared with four other women. As if that were not enough, caustic soda was out of stock for half a year in the only store that sold it, and caustic soda is absolutely essential in soapmaking. So my enthusiasm waned and I am not at all as active as before.

Then, ungratefully, Solomon Islands broke the diplomatic relations with Taiwan and began flirting with the People's Republic of China...

Economic equality

In contrast to Polynesia, which has hierarchical communities with hereditary chiefship, the communities in Melanesia are non-hierarchical. Chiefs are elected out of personal suitability. Leadership may also arise for specific purposes, so that somebody who is best at fishing becomes a temporary leader when it comes to fishing. A chief doesn't have to be omniscient or the best at everything.

Solomon Islands (as well as Melanesia in general) is thus in principle an egalitarian society. All inhabitants have the right to land in their home village and all are thereby landowners and economically equal. Some resources are scarce, but nobody is starving. There are no very rich and no very poor. Here exist no castes, no classes, no rich clans or families. What exist are more or less wealthy individuals. They are individuals that the whole family have chosen to invest in and pay for an education. They are in their turn obliged to help their relatives. Those wealthy individuals are distinguished by real shoes (instead of flip-flops) and little better clothes. And smartphones.

This economic equality has been described by Jared Diamond in his book *Guns, Germs and Steel*, with examples from Solomon Islands and Papua New Guinea. He pictures the traditional egalitarian social system in these two countries, where information and decision making are communal. There are no ranks or classes, and no individual can become outstandingly rich, since she or he will have social obligations to share. In a such traditional society, there are no bureaucrats, police or taxes. The economy is not built on any central distribution but on the mutual exchanging of necessities. This is in accordance with my own observations.

I need to point out that this applies to the traditional way of living, the kastom system. In the modern Solomon Islands, there are both bureaucrats and a police force. But still no excessively rich.

Back to Diamond. He again underlines that full-time specialists are lacking and that every member of the society has to do their lot in gathering, hunting and growing food. Since everybody is assumed to do all kinds of work, also dirty or unpleasant ones, not only specialists are lacking but also slaves.

Again, this system has been somewhat eliminated in the modern society. But the old kastom is still considered as the most honourable. Rhoda Sikilabu, whom I met at United Church Rest House in 2007 (see Part I), was met with great respect when she left her fancy life in Honiara in order to return to her village. She became a politician, but I guess she is still growing her own kumara.

Here there are no nursing homes for the elderly, no orphanages. Orphans, as well as children of unwed mothers, are taken care of by the family.

Begging is something very unusual. In my first visit in Honiara I did not see one single beggar. Now, over 14 years, I have seen two. They show their license that they have the right to sit and receive money. They are not shouting or stretching out their hand, just sitting, with a piece of cardboard carton on the ground with some coins.

Another culture?

Melanesia is, according to accessible information, very traditional and male chauvinistic, especially Malaita, especially the Kwaio. But this is not something I have noticed among my near and dear in Koa Hill, Honiara, or in my village Fousisigi in Malaita. Either my family and village are an exception, or one has to question the information or possibly redefine male chauvinism. For example, women sell goods at the market. The husband and wife can stay separate for a long time, while the wife attends to the business in the capital and the husband remains in the village. Unwed mothers don't meet any major problems.

The cultural differences between Solomon Islands and Sweden are negligible. The Solomon Islanders are somewhat like the Swedes. The most honoured virtues are a low voice and self-control rather than being loudmouthed, boisterous and aggressive. Conflicts within the group are traditionally solved by dialogue and negotiation between the parties. It is seen as inappropriate to highlight oneself; instead, the parties try to reach a consensual understanding which benefits everyone. Properties like honesty, group solidarity, modesty and humility are acclaimed.

With this follow inhibitions and fear of conflicts. As in Sweden, alcohol can be used as an excuse to release these inhibitions. Admittedly, many of these laudable virtues are breaking down. There are fiddlers and wranglers, loudmouths and violators. But still, these above-mentioned virtues are acclaimed, and those who violate them are looked down upon. This is no place for personal careerists or individualists.

Well, those two cultures – the Solomon and the Swedish – are not totally similar. Time concepts are different. 'Solomon time' means 'some time in the future'; it goes for personal meetings, official appointments and ships. (Airplanes are more specific, at least for international flights.) And the family units are *very* strong. In a country without any national social benefits, your family is your only guarantee. But these minor differences are almost always a delight for me. I have committed some minor breaches of protocol, although I should have known better, and there will surely be more. But since I showed that my mistake was unintended, people here are outstanding when it comes to tolerance and indulgence. I have never met any forms of cultural clash.

On a flight to Fiji I read an article in Air Pacific's travel magazine about an English woman married to a Fijian and living in Fiji. She 'adapted to Fijian lifestyle like a duck to water', they wrote, and this is the way I feel too. I interpret it as: I don't have to adapt at all, since this is the right life for me and a natural existence.

Development of society

Since my first arrival in 2006, there have been landslide developments, both societal and technological. The population growth of Solomon Islands and especially of Honiara is very high – albeit decreasing – which means high pressure on the capital's infrastructure: housing, medical care, education and so on. The traffic jams in Honiara are compact.

Photo 30

Also in Koa Hill, the area has been impacted by the population pressure. Five houses have become eight; the number of inhabitants has doubled and must share water and toilets. Sometimes friction. But usually, there is a natural fellowship: the children play together, the adults chat.

In 2006, whoever owned a mobile phone was a king. You had to go to a phone box and dial, using a phone card. Then they introduced a Top-up system, where you could pay a sum to an agent, e.g., a store or a private person, who thus recharged your mobile account. Now *everyone* (well, *almost* everyone) has a mobile phone, and even the children nag about a smartphone. Mobiles are made in China and relatively cheap. In 2006, you had to check your email or use the internet in internet cafés. Now, in 2020, you pay $6 and have free internet on your mobile for 24 hours. Most of those internet cafés have consequently closed down.

The telecommunication has not only improved in Honiara but also in the provinces. The two telephone companies, the national Our Telekom and the private BMobile, have built towers far away in the most remote islands. Before, in Robert's village, if you needed to communicate with the outside world, you had to use shortwave radio. Now we use our mobiles and connect to the web, just like that. Facebook is flourishing.

The country is dynamic and energetic (even though not all ideas are followed up). When I was a volunteer in the YWCA, I became aware of a great many activities; there are meetings and conferences and workshops and... The authorities are trying to tackle several serious issues. Contraception, HIV and domestic violence are talked about openly.

Honiara has had a facelift. At NPF Plaza, there used to be some traditional leaf huts with food kiosks. Now the stalls are pulled down to make way for modern, expensive shops, new shiny buffets and an Indian restaurant on the second floor. Pity, since the old plaza was the only place you could buy cooked local food. All other lunch spots are Chinese-owned and serve Chinese food. Which is delicious. But still.

Just alongside NPF Plaza is the National Museum, as previously mentioned. But in addition to the museum building itself, as well as offices, library and more, there is the newly built auditorium, an excellent place for film festivals, public speeches, lectures, presentations and other mass events.

In Commonwealth Street, between Mendana Avenue and the harbour, you can admire the newly erected Solomon Scouts & Coast-watcher's memorial, in honour of these war heroes. Another novelty is the Unity Square, with the highest flag pole in the Pacific. And my favourite café in the very centre of town, Amy's, has changed its name to Sky Horse Café.

Just in case you, reader, arrive in Honiara and want to see the places I have depicted.

Many fancy shopping centres have arisen, where there used to be empty lots or shabby little stores with walls reddened by betel nut spit. Public buildings like Our Telekom, Bank South Pacific and the Post Office have been transformed beyond recognition from small hovels to elegant spaces with air-conditioning. May Honiara never lose its soul.

Here I Live

There are no dramatic events here; life just goes on. Some earth quakes, floods, baby cyclones, riots, not worth mentioning... Being a housewife, a soap maker and a writer in Solomon Islands is no adventurous existence. You can hardly call it travelling or a journey either. It is surely not a journey in the sense that you move from one place to another. But it is definitely a journey in the sense of penetrating deep inside another culture.

In emails and Facebook-posts from Sweden everybody talks about 'autumn', 'winter' and 'snow'; it feels so strange and unreal. Since every day is more or less the same here, I can sense neither autumn nor winter. I find myself in an eternal summer. Here I have escaped from both pantyhose and autumn depressions.

Somebody said that I have proved that it is possible to live a happy life without status things one doesn't need. And here I do have everything I need: electricity (even if the solar panels sometimes go on the blink), clean running water, food from the market, fish and fruit of a quality you will never find in Sweden, goods from the innumerable Chinese stores.

Sometimes life here can be trying. The social obligations, the lack of privacy, the strict gender roles, the corruption which is creeping into daily life, and the slow pace when you want to get something done. If I were younger, I am not sure I would have managed it. In those days, I had much more rigid ideas of what life should be like. Life experience has made me more tolerant and flexible. And I would never have managed it without my husband Robert. He is broadminded, creative and driven. *And* a firm defender of kastom.

And these annoyances are a cheap price for what I have gained: Peace of heart and mind.

There are some foodstuffs in Sweden I appreciate when I am there (or in Australia), for example yoghurt and muesli for breakfast, apples, oranges. Here is too hot and humid even for oranges. But these are not things I miss when I am here.

The best thing I have done in my life was to sell all needless things that I owned. The money has gone to help family members with other needs. Buying nails for someone who wants to build their own house and not live with the parents-in-law, for example. Contributing to an airplane charter to send a dead body to the home village. Buying solar panels for the villagers so they don't have to sit in darkness after sunset. Paying school fees for talented youth who can study for a better future. In Sweden, it is so little money – in Solomon Islands it means the difference between a better life and a worse one.

Plans for the future? I don't have many plans. I'm satisfied with just going on... When we have the money, we will maybe build a new extension of the house... Maybe we will go to Sweden again, just for a visit. I don't think I will ever make it to South America. After my illness I am not as strong as before, and I can't see myself trekking in the Amazon rainforest, although I would like to. If I travel, I would rather go back to my old favourite 'hunting grounds' – e.g., Crete, Uganda, Cambodia, Tahiti – and show them to Robert. Since I have been there before I could compare my impressions with his.

I am sitting in the yard. In a while, there is *l'heure jaune*, 'the yellow hour', not *l'heure bleu*, 'the blue hour' like in Paris but *l'heure jaune* here in Koa Hill, Honiara, when the yellow twilight descends on the Mataniko River, where the magnificent coconut palms mirror themselves and the plastic bags are swimming, over humans and animals, over good and evil. The air is mild, people's movements are getting slower. The sky is on fire; the clouds are pink shifting towards orange. The sun has already set behind the hill with the American Memorial and Our Telekom's tower, which disturbs our TV signal. But let us forget about the negative elements now, and I feel that I will never, ever give this up. It will forever be a part of me.

# # #

AFTERWORD

In the year of 2020, the world was struck by the pandemic COVID-19 or Corona-virus. When it began to spread around the world, Solomon Islands was very fast to close the borders. Only some repatriation flights were arranged to bring home stranded Solomon Islanders abroad, e.g., students and seasonal workers from New Zealand, Australia, Fiji and Philippines. Those newly arrived had, and have, to spend two weeks in quarantine. In that way, Solomon Islands could remain one of the 10 nations in the world free from the virus for a long time.

In October 2020 the bomb burst. One of the repatriated students from overseas appeared COVID-19 positive. (He was tested negative before departure however.) He is at this moment still in isolation. A week later – yet another case. Government, Ministry of Health and Medical Services and other authorities seem fairly well prepared to meet this new threat, but the situation is unclear. The pandemic has serious impacts on the nation's economy and life in general.

Honiara 19 October 2020

PHOTOS

Photo 1
Flower pots
along Mendana
Avenue

Photo 2
Betel nuts for
sale

Photo 3
Panpipes and
musician in
traditional
dress

Photo 4
Metron Betari
preparing a
motu

Photo 5
Nguzunguzu

Photo 6
The dynamic
harbour

Photo 7
Two little
blondes

Photo 8
The raft across
Mataniko River

Photo 9
Our house

Photo 10
Robert and I
outside our
house

Photo 11
Sandra and Roy
cleaning *kasume*

Photo 12
Market!

Photo 13
Washing
clothes at the
third spring

Photo 14
Building the new
veranda

Photo 15
On board *L C
Dragon*

Photo 16
Sinaragu bay

Photo 17
Fousisigi at
high tide

Photo 18
Aunty
Kwaleka –
the rock

Photo 19
My late father-in-law Tome Arika, standing with his knapsack, trying to settle a dispute. Around 1975.

Photo 20
Common Christmas Supper

Photo 21
Rubaka making coconut milk

Photo 22
Odlian weaving
a basket from
coconut leaflets

Photo 23
Women among
the hidden
people weaving
baskets

Photo 24
Traditional
shell money
making

183

Photo 25
Men with shell jewellery at a culture festival

Photo 26
Bride price Langa Langa style

Photo 27
Our new house

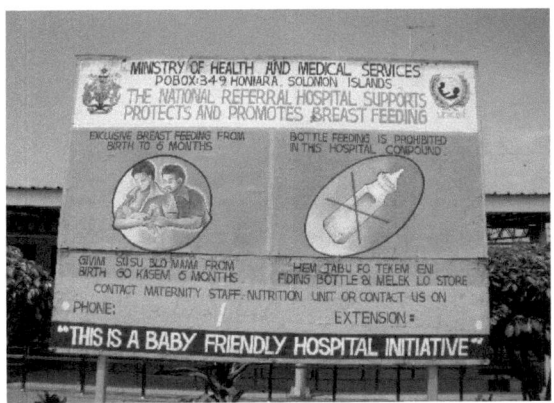

Photo 28
No bottle-feeding!

Photo 29
Sharing a tent stall with my craft colleague Naomi at Nautilus

Photo 30
New Honiara!

MAPS

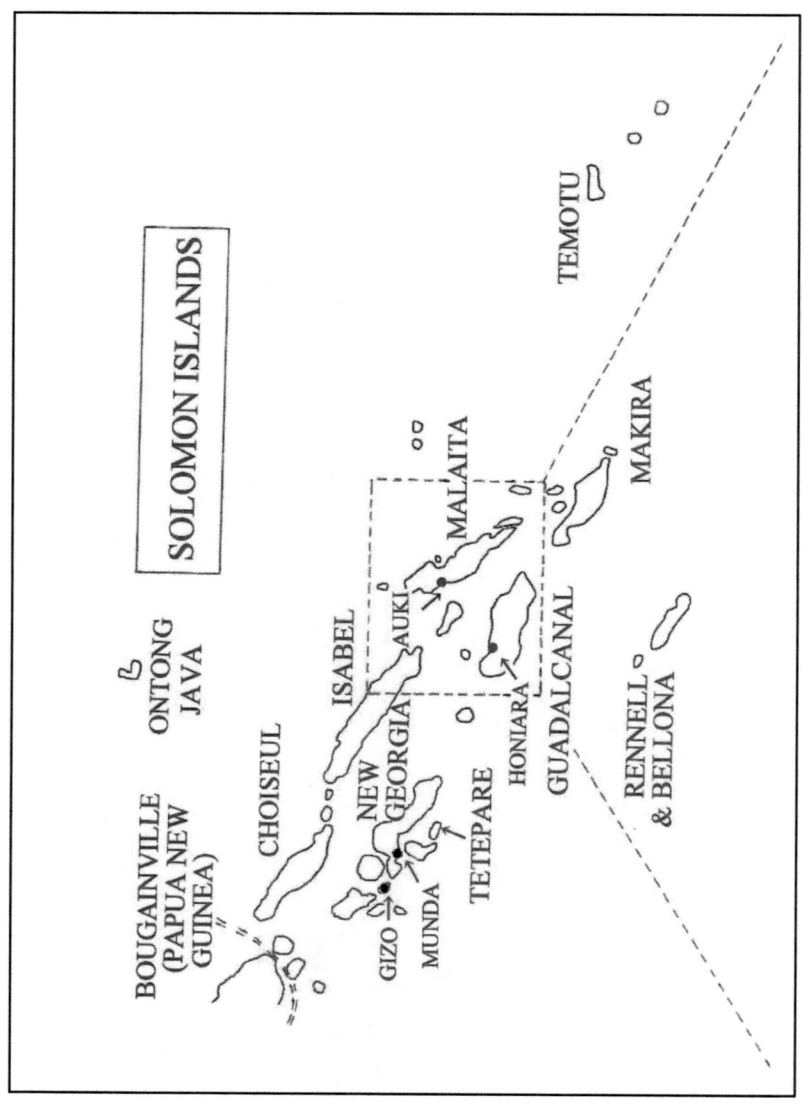

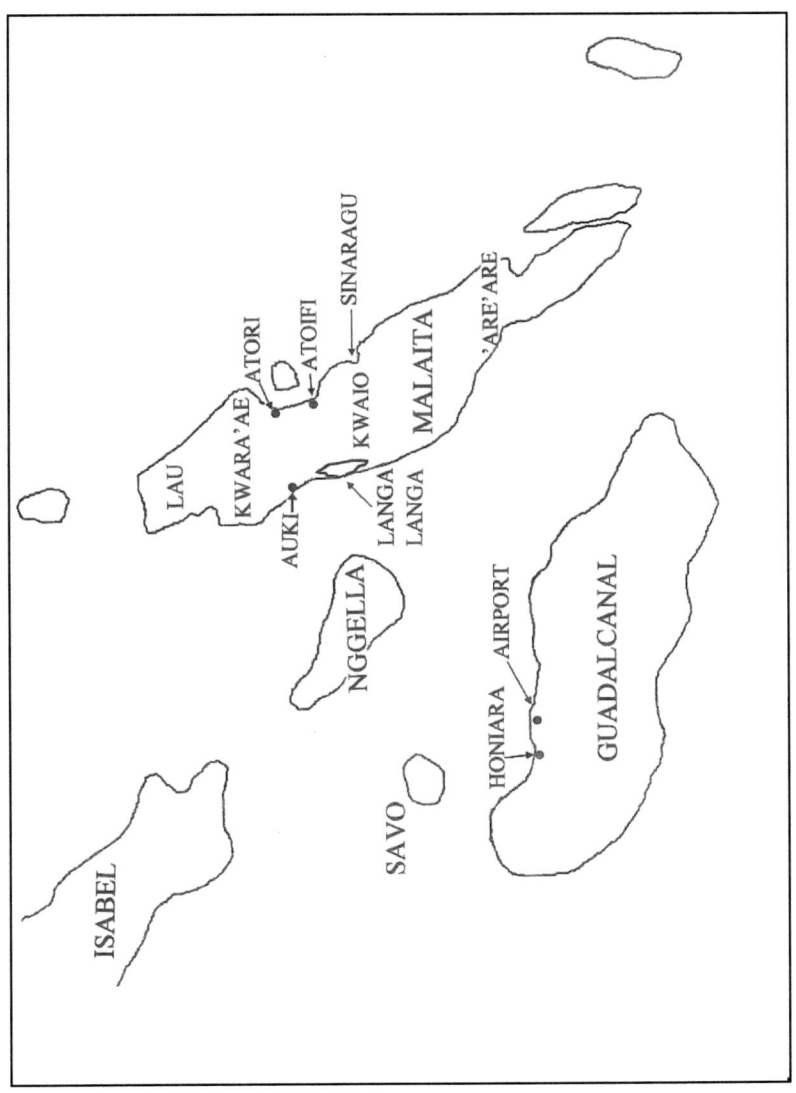

187

CONTACT THE AUTHOR

Ann Lindvall Arika

Facebook: *Ann Arika* http://facebook.com/ann.arika.545

Blog: *Soloblog* annlindvallarika.blogspot.com

OTHER RELEVANT PUBLICATIONS BY THE AUTHOR

Härhemma i Honiara – mitt liv i Salomonöarna [Here at Home in Honiara – My Life in Solomon Islands] Language: Swedish. Publisher: Nomen Förlag 2011

Glimpses of the Linguistic Situation in Solomon Islands. International Conference on Languages, E-Learning and Romanian Studies 2011

Korallbältet – resor i Melanesien och Mikronesien [The Coral Belt – Travelling in Melanesia and Micronesia] Language: Swedish. Publisher: Mekong Bokförlag 2008

Bananbältet – resor i Östafrika och Cuba [The Banana Belt – Travelling in East Africa and Cuba] Co-author: Tore Gulbrandsen. Language: Swedish. Publisher: Mekong Bokförlag 2006

Det gröna Tioman [The Green Tioman] In: *15 gånger Asien* [15 Times Asia] Language: Swedish. Publisher: Mekong Bokförlag 2006

Transitivity in Discourse – A Comparison of Greek, Polish and Swedish. Language: English. Ph.D. thesis. Publisher: Lund University Press 1998